D0918602

BEACHEY, R. W. The slave trade of Eastern Africa. Barnes & Noble, a div. of Harper & Row, 1976. 324p maps bibl index 76-377944.
18.00 ISBN 0-06-490326-5
BEACHEY, R. W. A collection of documents on The slave trade of Eastern Africa. Barnes & Noble, a div. of Harper & Row, 1976.
140p map index 76-15785. 11.00 ISBN 0-06-490328-1

Whereas the Atlantic slave trade has been carefully studied, little has been done on the East African slave trade. Beachey's two-volume study, therefore, is a welcome addition. The first volume, Beachey's analysis and interpretation of primary and secondary sources, is a general survey for antiquity to the 19th century. A regional analysis is preferred. Beachey also discusses some political and social repercussions of the trade in the interior. Attempting a quantitative estimate, he suggests that for the 19th century alone, approximately 2.2 million slaves were sold. The second volume, a collection of documents from antiquity (which focus mainly on the 19th century), provides contemporary perspectives on the East African slave trade. Although this survey fills a gap in the literature, it lacks the criticism necessary in an area that is just being opened up for investigation. It also lacks the immediacy of the fieldwork approach and essential interdisciplinary

perspectives. Recommended for undergraduate and graduate reading in conjunction with more critical treatments, such as Edward A. Alpers's *Ivory and slaves* (CHOICE, Dec. 1975).

LARRY A. JACKSON LIBRARY
Lander College
Greenwood, S. C. 29646

A COLLECTION OF DOCUMENTS ON
The Slave Trade of Eastern Africa

A COLLECTION OF
DOCUMENTS
ON

The Slave Trade of Eastern Africa

R. W. BEACHEY

115055

REX COLLINGS LONDON 1976

LARRY A. JACKSON LIBRARY
Lander College
Greenwood, S. C. 29646

First published by Rex Collings Ltd
69 Marylebone High Street London W1

SBN 086036000 8

© Rex Collings Ltd 1976

Typeset by Malvern Typesetting Services
and printed in Great Britain
at the University Printing House, Cambridge
(Euan Phillips, University Printer)

CONTENTS

ACKNOWLEDGEMENTS

Acknowledgement is due to Dr. L. W. Hollingsworth for permission to quote from his book *Zanzibar under the Foreign Office 1890–1913* (Macmillan, London, 1953) (pages 158-9), the passage reproduced on pages 132-3 of this *Collection of Documents*. Acknowledgement is also due to the Seven Pillars Trust and Jonathan Cape Ltd., for permission to quote from T. E. Lawrence's *Seven Pillars of Wisdom* (Jonathan Cape Ltd., London, 1935) (page 89), and reproduced on pages 79-80 of this *Collection of Documents*. I wish to record my deepest thanks to Dr. G. S. P. Freeman-Grenville for generously making available to me photostat copies of documents from the French Archives.

PREFACE

This Collection of Documents is the by-product of research towards a separate and larger study, *The Slave Trade of Eastern Africa* (Rex Collings, London, 1976), and might be said to act as a Companion volume to that study. A number of the same extracts appear in both books. But the *Collection,* in contrast to the historical work, provides a picture of the Slave Trade of Eastern Africa as seen wholly through records which have been selected for the sense of reality and immediacy they give to what was a very important part of African and wider human history.

ABBREVIATIONS USED IN THE SOURCES

C	Command paper
Cd.	Command paper (old series)
Cmd.	Command paper (new series)
FO	Foreign Office
FOCP	Foreign Office Confidential Print
SP	Sessional Papers (British Parliamentary)

INTRODUCTION

The documents collected herein pertain mainly to the slave trade of
Eastern Africa in the nineteenth century. But the history of that trade
extends back into early millenia. There is brief skimped reference to
it in the annals of the eighteenth dynasty, in the reign of Thutmose
III, 1504–1450 BC, where it is recorded that 'slaves, male and
female', were brought back to Egypt from the land of Punt (present-
day Somaliland);[1] and negro slaves are depicted in Alexandrian
terracottas of the Ptolemaic period.[2] And, as we shall see in our first
document, the *Periplus of the Erythraean Sea,* of the early second
century AD, slaves of the better sort were brought back to Egypt from
the East African coast.[3] A treaty of the seventh century AD with
Nubia, which placed Egypt's southern boundary at the First
Cataract, also secured for her the continued supply of slaves from
Nubia.

Slavery appears to have been accepted as a natural institution, the
under-pinning of society, part and parcel of the historical process, in
the ancient world; and eastern Africa played a considerable role in
supporting it with a supply of slaves. This role continued when,
following the rise of Islam in the seventh century, there was increased
Arab contact with the East African coast. According to the
Portuguese writer, de Barros, the Arabs

> after they absorbed that infernal doctrine, which they upheld with the
> arms whose use Mohammed and the Khalifa who followed him had
> taught them; became much bolder and went much farther.[4]

And the *Kitab al-Ajaib al-Hind*, of the mid-tenth century, one of our
earliest documents of the early Islamic period, states that visitors to
East Africa from Oman preyed on its inhabitants, and they

> steal their children enticing them away by offering them fruits. They
> carry the children from place to place and finally take possession of them
> and carry them off to their own country.[5]

Chinese writings of the medieval period, in referring to lands in the
west, state that their inhabitants are black and that the Arabs take
slaves back from there to their own country; and these slaves when

[1] Breasted, J. H., *Ancient Records of Egypt*, New York, Vol. II, 1906,
p. 204.
[2] Fraser, P. M., *Ptolemaic Alexandria*, London, Vol. I, 1972, p. 74.
[3] Frisk, H. (ed) *Le Périple de la Mer Erythrée*, Göteberg, 1927.
[4] de Barros, J., *Decadas da Asia*, I, (ed. A. Baiao), Coimbra, 1938.
[5] van der Lith, P. A. *Kitab al-Ajaib al-Hind*, Leiden, 1883–6, p. 22.

taken to China are worth their weight in aromatic wood.[1]

The presence of large numbers of East African slaves in the lower Euphrates Valley and in India during the Middle Ages would indicate a long-standing slave trade with the East African coast. East African slaves were in sufficient strength in the Euphrates Valley to capture Basra in 869 AD, and to continue their ravages there for a number of years. In Bengal, in the late fifteenth century, they temporarily set up their own regime. These slave populations overseas were fed by a slave trade on the East African coast. Ibn Battuta, who visited Kilwa in the fourteenth century, noted that its Sultan led frequent raids against Africans on the mainland; and slaves were so plentiful that the Sultan and son presented twenty of them to an indigent fakir from the Yemen. Slaves were a stock-in-trade for which there was always demand.

The arrival of the Portuguese on the East African coast at the end of the fifteenth century brought a rigid monopoly of trade, breached by the Arabs only on Portuguese sufferance. And thus, although a description of Kilwa in 1505 might record that

> There are more black slaves than white Moors here; they are engaged on farms growing maize and other things,[2]

the slave trade on the East African coast declined in importance under Portuguese rule. Not that the Portuguese were indifferent to it. Evidence is all to the contrary. But the paramount interest of the Portuguese lay in India. East Africa was important to them only insofar as it lay on the route to India. Domestic slaves might sometimes be carried to India by the Portuguese (there are accounts of them falling into English, Dutch, and Turkish hands from captured Portuguese ships), and Alexander Hamilton states that

> The King's ships, as well as private traders, bring good store of them to India, both sexes being in high esteem with the Indian Portuguese[3]

But, on the whole, India did not offer a market for African slaves. There was ample cheap low-class labour in India without need to import slaves from abroad. Nor did the Portuguese carry slaves to the Islamic countries of the Middle East: their Christian religion forbade this. For did not slaves usually adopt the religion of their masters!

---

[1] Duvenydak, J. L. L., *China's Discovery of Africa*, London, 1949, pp. 13-14, p. 22.
[2] Axelson, E., *South-East Africa 1488-1530*, London, 1940, pp. 231-8.
[3] Hamilton (Captain), Alexander, *A New Account of the East Indies*, Edinburgh, 1727, Vol. 1, p. 10.

A few slaves were carried around the Cape; but even after 1645, when their export from East Africa to Brazil was permitted by Portugal, the traffic never amounted to much. The long haul and boisterous waters of the Cape made it a dangerous and expensive proposition. Not until a later age of faster ships and diminished supplies from West Africa did it assume importance.

By the mid-seventeenth century the Portuguese were increasingly challenged by the Omani Arabs, the Dutch, English and French. By 1650, they had been ejected from Muscat and the Arabian seaboard; and by 1740 their great stronghold, Fort Jesus, at Mombasa, had fallen to the Arabs. By the mid-eighteenth century, they had given up control of the coastal strip north of the Ruvuma river. The Omani Arabs re-asserted their political and commercial dominion in the wake of Portuguese withdrawal. The slave trade again took on significant proportions. The French also for a time, in the later eighteenth century, resorted to the East African coast for slave labour for their developing sugar industry in their possessions in the Indian Ocean. In 1776, they entered into an arrangement with the Sultan of Kilwa for a regular supply of slaves, but the onset of the French Revolution frustrated this scheme.

During the eighteenth century there is little evidence of British interest in the East African coast. A visit by Captain James Lancaster, of the *Edward Bonaventure,* to Zanzibar in 1592, and a three-months stopover there for repairs and provisioning which brought the report that Zanzibar

> for the goodenesse of the harborough and watering, and plentifull refreshing with fish, whereof we tooke great store with our nets, and for sundry sorts of fruits of the countrey, as cocos and others, which were brought to us by the Moores, as also for oxen and hennes, is carefully to be sought for by such of our ships, as shall hereafter passe that way,[1]

was not followed up. Ships bound for India, after rounding the Cape, tended to strike northeast to the south of Zanzibar; there was little inducement to run up to that island, possibly in the face of an adverse current and wind. Not until the Napoleonic wars and the need to forestall the French in East African waters did the British look to the East African coast.

Lieutenant Bissell of the *Leopard,* who visited Zanzibar in 1799, noted that 'There had not been an English ship in Zanzibar within the memory of the oldest inhabitant'.[2] The French however had been

---

[1] R. Hakluyt's *Principal Navigations,* Hakluyt Society, 1904, Vol. VI, pp. 392–5.

[2] Bissell, A. *A Voyage from England to the Red Sea 1798-9,* London, 1806, pp. 31–7.

frequent visitors there for some years, and as a consequence many of the inhabitants could speak French. Bissell also noted the annual visitation of the northern Arabs. Trading vessels from the Persian Gulf, after discharging their cargoes, usually dates, laid up at Zanzibar, awaiting the onset of the southwest monsoons to embark their cargo of slaves for the north. It was a familiar pattern, one which was to dominate the nineteenth century history of the East African coast; and the subject of which is the concern of most of the documents in this collection.

I
THE ANCIENT AND
MEDIEVAL WORLD

The *Periplus of the Erythraean Sea*, a form of super-cargo's guide, by an anonymous author, probably from Alexandria, and probably written about the early second century AD, is our earliest document referring to the slave trade on the East African coast south of Cape Guardafui. It appears to have been based on a first-hand knowledge of the coast and its products, and indicates that the Arabs already had ancient contact with the coast by this date. The following extract is from a translation from the Greek text in H. Frisk, *Le Périple de la Mer Erythrée*, Göteborg, 1927, pp.5-6 quoted in G. S. P. Freeman-Grenville, *The East African Coast, Select Documents*, London, 1962, pp. 1-2. Opone referred to here is probably the site of present-day Ras Hafun.

From Tabai after 400 stades sailing is a promontory towards which the current runs, and the market-town of Opone . . . It produces cinnamon, both the *aroma* and *moto* varieties, as well as the better sort of slaves, which are brought to Egypt in increasing numbers, and much tortoiseshell of better quality than elsewhere . . . After Opone the coast veers more towards the south . . . Men of the greatest stature, who are pirates, inhabit the whole coast and at each place have set up chiefs. The Chief of the Ma'afir is the suzerain, according to an ancient right which subordinates it to the kingdom which has become the first in Arabia. The people of Mouza hold it in tribute under his sovereignty and send there small ships, mostly with Arab captains and crews who trade and intermarry with the mainlanders of all the places and know their language.

CHINESE SOURCES ON THE EAST AFRICAN SLAVE TRADE IN THE NINTH AND TWELFTH CENTURIES

There is no evidence of direct Chinese contact with the East African coast, although with their large ships and knowledge of navigation this would have been possible. It is more likely that their knowledge of and trade with East Africa came indirectly through transhipment of trade from Southeast Asia. The following extracts are taken from Duyvendak, J. J. L., *China's Discovery of Africa*, London, 1949, pp. 13-14, pp. 22-3.
     The Chinese scholar, Tuan Ch'eng-shih, who died in 863 AD, in the *Yu-yang-tsa-tsu*, states that

The country of Po-pa-li is in the southwestern sea. (The people) do not eat any of the five grains but eat only meat. They often stick a needle into the veins of cattle and draw blood which they drink raw, mixed with milk. They wear no clothes except that they cover (the parts) below their loins with sheepskins. Their women are clean and of proper behaviour. The inhabitants themselves kidnap them, and if they sell them to foreign merchants, they fetch several times their price. The country produces only ivory and ambergris. If Persian merchants wish to go into their country, they collect around them several thousand men and present them with strips of cloth. All, whether old or young draw blood and swear an oath, and then only do they trade their products. From olden times they were not subject to any foreign country. In fighting they use elephants' tusks and ribs and the horns of wild buffaloes as lances and they wear cuirasses and bows and arrows. They have twenty myriads of foot soldiers. The Arabs make frequent raids upon them.

And Chou Ch'u-fei, who wrote the *Ling-wai-tai-ta*, in 1178, states (possibly referring to Zanzibar or Madagascar) that in the west

there is an island in the sea on which there are many savages. Their bodies are black as lacquer and they have frizzled hair. They are enticed by (offers of) food and then captured and sold as slaves to the Arabic countries, where they fetch a very high price. They are employed as gate-keepers, and it said that they have no longing for their kinsfolk. . . . thousands of them are sold as foreign slaves.

AN ARABIC ACCOUNT OF A TENTH CENTURY SLAVING VENTURE

In a collection of sailors' tales, the *Kitab al-Ajaib al-Hind*, by a Persian Gulf sailor, Buzurg, of the tenth century, an account of a slaving venture takes an unusual turn. A party of Omani sailors are driven by a storm on to the East African coast. They are welcomed by the local ruler, who assists them in their trading activities. The following account is taken from G. S. P. Freeman-Grenville, *The East African Coast, Select Documents*, London, 1962, pp. 9–13, translated from P. A. van der Lith, *Kitab al-Ajaib al-Hind*, Leiden, 1883-6, pp. 50-60.

When everything was in order, and the king knew of our intention to set sail, he accompanied us to the shore with several of his people, got into one of the boats and came out to the ship with us. He even came on board with seven of his companions.

When I saw them there, I said to myself: In the Oman market this young king would certainly fetch thirty dinars, and his seven companions sixty dinars. Their clothes alone are not worth less than twenty dinars. One way and another this would give us a profit of at least 3,000 dirhams, and without any trouble. Reflecting thus, I gave

the crew their orders. They raised the sails and weighed anchor
. . . When the day came, the king and his companions were
put with the other slaves whose number reached about 200 head. He
was not treated differently from his companions in captivity. The king
said not a word and did not even open his mouth. He behaved as if we
were unknown to him and as if we did not know him. When he got to
Oman, the slaves were sold, and the king with them.

After several years in captivity, during which he becomes a convert to
Islam, the ruler manages to find his way back to his homeland. Shortly
after this, the adventurers who had previously enslaved him are again
driven by a storm on to his coast; and to their dismay find themselves in
the power of him whom they had previously betrayed. But such is the
comity of Islam that all is forgiven.

We said farewell to him. Go, he said, and if you return, I shall not
treat you otherwise than I have done. You will receive the best
welcome. And the Muslims may know that they may come here to us,
as to brothers, Muslims like themselves. As for accompanying you to
your ship, I have reasons for not doing so. And on that we parted.

The above is important in showing that there was already a market and
established value for East African slaves in Oman by the tenth century.

II
FRENCH AND PORTUGUESE SLAVERS

The slave trade carried on by French and Portuguese slavers on the southern portion of the East African coast was of comparatively short duration, confined mainly to the latter years of the eighteenth century and first half of the nineteenth century. It was at its height at the time of Captain Owen's visit to Quelimane during the early 1820s. Thereafter it dwindled, until by the mid-nineteenth century it was completely overshadowed by the dominant Arab slave trade to the north.

The following, quoted by G. S. P. Freeman-Grenville, *The French at Kilwa Island*, London, 1965, pp. 83-4, describes the arrangement to supply slaves from Kilwa for the French possessions in the Indian Ocean. It proved to be abortive, owing to the outbreak of the French Revolution and lack of backing from the French government.

We, King of Kilwa, Sultan Hasan, son of Sultan Ibrahim and son of Sultan Yusuf the Shirazi, Kilwa, give our word to Monsieur Morice, a French national, that we will provide him with 1,000 slaves a year for twenty *piastres* each and that he will give the king a tribute of two *piastres* per head of slaves. No other than he shall be able to trade for slaves, be he French, English, Dutch, Portuguese, &c., unless and until he [sc. Monsieur Morice] shall have received his slaves and requires no more. This contract is made for 100 years between him and us. To guarantee our word we give him the fortress in which he can place the number of cannons he desires and his flag. The French, the Moors and the King of Kilwa will henceforward be one. Whosoever attacks one of us we two together will attack him.

    Made on 14 December 1776 under our signs and seals,
    signed: Morice.

And further down is written:

We the undersigned Captain and Officers of the vessel *L'Abyssinie*, owner Monsieur Morice, certify to all whom it may concern that the present treaty was made in our presence at Kilwa on 14 December 1776.

    Signed: Pichard, Pigne, Broüard.

These notes by a slaving captain, Joseph Crassons de Medeuil, who ranged along the coast of what is present day Mozambique, and as far north as Kilwa, are taken from G. S. P. Freeman-Grenville, *The East African Coast, Select Documents*, London, 1962, pp. 192-7.

The stretch between Mozambique and Ibo is fairly thickly

populated. It is there we go in search of our blacks. We trade for them at Kerimba, Ibo and Mozambique, small islands detached from the coast and inaccurately marked on the map.

From Cape Delgado to Kilwa the coast is inhabited only by Moors and Arabs who take from it a prodigious number of blacks (*in margin:* inferior to those of Kilwa but which they bring there to sell to us), particularly from the river Mongallo, a little-known river which flows through fertile and thickly populated country stretching a long way inland.

. . . . this country produces millet, indigo, superb cotton, silkier even than the cotton produced on the Ile de Bourbon, sugar cane, gums in abundance, brown cowries of the second sort which are currency at Jiddah and in Dahomey, besides elephant ivory which is very common, as are elephants, and lastly negroes — superb specimens if they are selected with care. This selection we cannot make ourselves, being at the discretion of the traders, who are now aware of our needs and who know that it is absolutely essential for us to sail at a given season in order to round the Cape of Good Hope. In addition to competition amongst ourselves the expeditions have never been properly thought out and always left to chance, and so it happens that three or four ships find themselves in the same place and crowd each other out. This would not happen if there were a properly organized body and the expeditions were planned to fit in with the seasons and the quantity of cargo and the means of using up surplus also planned, since it is not the business of seamen to concern themselves with correspondence and administration. To my knowledge, the trading that has been done in this port for the last three years, without counting traders not personally known to me, is as follows:

La Pintade	Capt		600	blacks
La Victoire	,,	La Touche	224	,, 1st voyage
Les bons amis	,,	Beguet	336	,,
La Samaritaine	,,	Herpin	254	,,
La Créolle	,,	Crassons	176	,,
La Victoire	,,	La Touche 3rd voyage 230 }	690	,, In his three ,, voyages
[omitted]	,,	Berton	233	,,
La Grande Victoire	,,	Michel	289	,,
La Thémis	,,	Bertau	450	
La Grande Victoire	,,	Michel	289	,,
La Créolle	,,	Crassons	211	,,
La Thémis 2nd voyage	,,	Bertau	480	,,

La Gde. Victoire	Capt. Rouillard	250 blacks
		— ,,
		4,193 ,,

A total, to my knowledge, of 4,193, and certainly there must have been more in three years.

> Captain W. F. Owen, who during the course of a survey of the East African coast, 1822-4, visited the port of Quelimane, noted in his *Narrative of Voyages to Explore the Eastern Shores of Africa*, London, 1833, vol. i, pp. 292-3.

From eleven to fourteen slave vessels come annually from Rio de Janeiro to this place, and return with four to five hundred slaves each on an average. They are purchased with blue dungaree, coloured cloths, arms, gun powder, brass and pewter, red coloured beads in imitation of coral, cutlery and various other articles. The free blacks of the country and *banyans* carry on the trade inland for their merchants: and the arrival of one of these people among the tribes with his pedlar's stock is the signal for the general warfare when the weak become the victim of the strong. To contain the slaves collected for sale every Portuguese house has an extensive yard or enclosure, called a barracon, generally surrounded by a lofty brick wall.

> In 1843 Lieutenant Barnard of the *Cleopatra* seized the *Progresso*, a well-known slaver, near Quelimane after a seven-hour chase. The *Progresso* only hove to when musketry reached her sails, and following the capture, according to Lieutenant Barnard, RN, *Three Years Cruise in the Mozambique Channel for Suppression of the Slave Trade*, London, 1848, p. 40,

the slaves broke adrift and broke open the casks of *aqua ardiente*, which some of them drank in large quantities: others took salt water, salt beef and pork and raw fowls, in consequence of which fifty died the first night, which unfortunately was squally; to save the vessel the poor wretches were obliged to be kept below or run the risk of being washed overboard.

A few days later

We saw poor sickly skeletons lying on the deck, evidently dying and much disfigured by having been trodden on or crushed underneath by the others: they could just gasp, and now and then open their lips whilst an orange was squeezed on them. The others were all covered with craw-craws and itch, and were scratching large sores all over their bodies and howling like maniacs for water. I went on the slave deck, and half the blacks were then on it, who gave their sign of welcome by clapping their hands in concert.

Commander Wyvill, Commander-in-Chief at the Cape, reported in 1852

I regret that the Portuguese authorities instead of repressing this traffic, afford every facility for its continuance. I learn that the Governor of Inhambane permitted a slaver to lie at anchor off that port for three weeks and capture 1000 slaves in December 1851, and that the Governor of Ibo connived at the trade.

SP XXXIX 1852/53, Select Committee Report: Q 1627

The following extract from *The Observer*, Monday, 22 February 1819 — and quoted in *The Observer*, Sunday, 23 February 1969 — pertains to the slave trade that was carried on with Mauritius from the East African mainland, although Mauritius was then (1819) in British hands.

Philip Caday, alias Phillibert, Amand Clarensac, and Joseph Ann Tregrosse, were arraigned at the Old Bailey on Saturday to take trial for having feloniously taken a number of Negroes from the Mozambique Islands, on the coast of Africa, and carried them to the Isle de France, in the Mauritius, for the purpose of being dealt with as slaves, contrary to the statute etc. The *Magicienne* frigate was stationed off the Isle of France to suppress the traffic in slaves. The captain saw a schooner, of which the prisoners were part of the crew, in the harbour, and suspected it was in the slave trade. He sent some of his men in pursuit and it was discovered that 92 human beings had been landed for the purpose of sale. The prisoners were afterwards apprehended. They were found guilty and sentenced to three years' confinement in the House of Correction, and to hard labour.

III
THE SLAVE TRADE BASED ON ZANZIBAR

It appears to have come almost as a revelation to many persons in England, as the following account from Captain P. Colomb's *Slave Catching in the Indian Ocean, A Record of Naval Experiences*, London, 1873, pp. 21-4, will show, that an extensive slave trade was carried on along the East African coast, and that it was based almost entirely on Zanzibar. However other accounts included here will show that other observers had noted the role of Zanzibar in this trade quite early in the century.

I well remember how, meeting once, years ago, a very celebrated and successful slave catcher, lately from the command of one of Her Majesty's ships in these waters, I was utterly astounded to learn that a traffic I supposed entirely restricted to the coast of Africa and the new world, was in much more active progress between East Africa and the northern shores of the Indian Ocean. At that time books of East African travel were not many; and popular knowledge of slave trading connected itself almost exclusively with the west coast of Africa. What went on in the east was neither understood nor thought of much importance. The waters of the Arabian Sea were under the management and dominion of the Indian Government; and being so, were left, as all things Indian are, to Indian views. The suppression of slave traffic was the child of British policy, and did not form a leading feature in that of our Indian empire. There was trouble enough already in managing so vast a continent, and an outside question, such as the slave trade, was left to take care of itself.

Now, however, Livingstone, Baker, Burton, Speke and Grant — and still more, recent transactions and writings — have familiarised the public mind with the idea of an extensive and flourishing man trade in Eastern Africa; and the methods of dealing with it at sea have passed from Indian into Imperial hands. But, judging from my own experience, there is still only a very vague notion of the nature, objects, and issues of the traffic. Its history must be gathered from stray passages in voluminous books of travel; in still more voluminous blue books, or in the reports of commissions. Of the sea traffic, the naval officer — after his manner — has written officially, but not for the public; and from him alone can such information come.

Zanzibar, the capital of the Arab kingdom south of the Line, the centre of trade in Eastern Africa, is the reservoir into which the trickling streams of black blood from the interior flow and are gathered, pending the opening of the sluices which permit its outlet to seaward. From 10,000 to 20,000 slaves are annually passed through Zanzibar territory, who find their final domicile in the dominions of the Sultan; on the shores, or in the interior of Arabia and Persia; or get a temporary resting-place on the decks of some British man-of-war, to be ultimately herded together at the Seychelles, at Bombay, or at Aden—sometimes as great a trouble to the authorities of those settlements, as ever their brethren in colour have proved to our transatlantic neighbours.

The winds and currents in the balanced ebb and flow which characterises their motions in the Indian Ocean, are the great regulators of native traffic, and of the slave season. The science of navigation, which permits the western merchant to despatch his wares at all seasons to all ports, and enables the mariner to dash boldly out where there is neither path nor trail, has not yet greatly invaded the unchanging east. The Arab feels safest within sight of land, and seldom dares to accept what we seek for 'plenty of sea room.' Thus he can only make his way at sea when there is such wind and current as shall carry his vessel in the roundabout direction involved in a coasting voyage.

The monsoons are consequently responsible for the Arab slave trade, and without them it must cease, as, in their absence it could probably never have arisen.

One of our first descriptions of the slave trade at Zanzibar is by Captain P. Dallons in 1804, who complains of the difficulty in negotiation with local authorities at Zanzibar for a supply of slaves. This extract is quoted in G. S. P. Freeman-Grenville, *The East African Coast, Select Documents*, p. 199.

Black slaves are sold by auction amid the shouts of public auctioneers. It is between these and the interpreter that takes place the commercial arrangements which ruin the French. They put up the price of the blacks at will, and end by making us fear that we shall not obtain them at any price, because their religion, as they say, forbids them in such a case to sell to white men. If one complains to the Arab government, it gives every appearance of hastening one's business; but matters none the less remain in their original state, until, at length, driven by one difficulty and another, we reach the conclusion of our trading. It is then that the Governor comes on board ship to count the blacks, and makes us pay dues of eleven *piastres* a head. Once the dues are paid the Governor overwhelms the

French with offers of his services, which may be reduced to that at least no further present will be demanded.

The inhabitants of the country trade in blacks as follows: they transport them to different markets, to Muscat, the Red Sea, and the Persian Gulf; and, although for this reason they can hardly fear our joining in the trade, above all because they pay only one *piastre* a head, they do all they can to keep us away from the island. Both the interests and the policy of the Prince of Muscat call us to it, and for certain the governors carry out neither the one nor the other.

By 1804, under Omani hegemony, Zanzibar was already the principal centre for the coastal slave trade. The slave market in Zanzibar was one of the sights of the town for visitors. We have here a number of accounts of it by Europeans. The first is that of Captain Thomas Smee, of the Bombay Marine, who in 1811 carried out a voyage of research in the western Indian Ocean, including a visit to Zanzibar, and recorded it in *Voyage to the Eastern Shores of Africa*, London, 1811.

The show commences about four o'clock in the afternoon. The slaves, set off to the best advantage by having their skins cleaned and burnished with coconut oil, their faces painted with red and white stripes, which is here esteemed elegance, and the hands, noses, ears, and feet, ornamented with a profusion of bracelets of gold and silver jewels, are arranged in a line commencing with the youngest, and increasing in the rear accordingly to their size and age. At the head of this file, which is composed of all sexes and ages from six to sixty, walks the person who owns them; behind and at each side two or three of his domestic slaves, armed with swords or spears, serve as a guard. Thus ordered, the procession begins, and as it passes through the market place and principal streets, the owner holding forth in a kind of song the good qualities of his slaves and the high prices that have been offered for them. When any of them strikes a spectator's fancy, the procession stops and a process of examination ensues, which for minuteness is unequalled in any cattle market in Europe. The intending purchaser, having ascertained that there is no defect in the facilities of speech, and hearing, that there is no disease present, and that the slave does not snore in sleeping, which is counted a very great fault, next proceeds to examine the person: the mouth and teeth are first inspected, and afterwards every part of the body in succession, not even excepting the breasts, etc., of the girls, many of whom I have seen examined in the most indecent manner in the public market by their purchasers; indeed there is every reason to believe that the slave dealers almost universally force the young females to submit to their lust previous to their being disposed of. The slave is then made to walk or run a little way to show that there is no defect about the feet; after which, if the price is agreed to, they are stripped of their finery and delivered over to their future master. I have frequently counted between twenty and thirty of these files in the market at one time, some of which contained about thirty (slaves). Women with children newly born hanging at their breasts and others so old they can scarcely walk, are sometimes seen dragged about in this manner. I observed they had in general a very dejected look; some groups appeared so ill fed that their bones seemed as if ready to penetrate the skin.

Another account of the Zanzibar slave market appears in Captain Colomb's *Slave-Catching in the Indian Ocean,* pp. 390-402.

The chief object of attraction to every Englishman on first reaching Zanzibar is undoubtedly the slave market . . .

. . . I was not half-an-hour on shore at Zanzibar before I wended my steps in this direction, and have now to set down what I saw.

The fairly clean courts and alleys of the European quarter of the town, with their smooth pavements, soon gave place to a series of stony watercourses, partly choked with rubbish and filth, winding in and out amongst stone houses, ruined walls, crumbled masonry, and mat huts. The way led in a few minutes to a small open space of irregular shape, with a flooring composed of decayed garden stuff, stones, and mud, in unequal proportions.

There was a good deal of black cattle on hand this evening, but the market was apparently dull, and prices ranged low; I believe, however, I was early for business. There might have been perhaps 250 head on sale, and these were for the most part seated in the open. Grown-up males and females were separated. Some were ranged in long rows, with their legs stretched out before them; others, chiefly men and boys, squatted in small groups and chatted amongst themselves. The owners, or persons in charge of the several groups, stood near each, talking quietly to them, or to their acquaintances amongst the crowd. Sometimes there was an inquiry about some particular individual in a group, and he or she would stand up and speak a few words in reply to questions. I saw the person in charge of a group of boys—he was a young Arab with some black blood in him—call one of them up and ask him some questions; then he looked narrowly at his eyes, and then placing his hand on his head raised the boy's eyelid with his thumb in precisely the same way as I have seen Dr Chlorodyne raise my boy's eyelid when there was a sty in it; I also saw the boy dismissed to his seat with something very like a kindly pat on the head.

There were a large number of Arab gentlemen, merchants and business men, present, who lounged through the groups of slaves, pointing them out occasionally with the inevitable little cane or stick which every Arab with any pretensions to gentility always carries.
. . . .

My guide now pointed to a slave then in process of sale, and we went over to the spot. The article was female; fat and strong, but not well favoured as to beauty. Indeed, to speak truth I doubt whether a face over which a curry-comb has apparently been drawn, could exactly be considered beautiful in our view. But the process of being made 'beautiful for ever' is a simple one in these parts; and a good sound scarification in early youth gives the cheeks and forehead a delightful resemblance to a ploughed field, which is so very permanent that no negro husband need be much afraid of a black Madam Rachel's bills in after-life.

The seller of this piece of goods was a bullet-headed, round-faced, dark Arab, who rested his arm lightly on the damsel's shoulder, and leaned lazily against a post. Bids were few and far between, and his auctioneering was drowsy work.

'Eighteen dollars, eighteen dollars,' drawled our friend, using the Swahili equivalent of the English words, 'eight-een — dol-lars.'

He will certainly fall asleep in the middle of the last word.

A gentleman strolls past in his flowing robes —

'What's the price?'

'Eight-een dollars. Eight-een. Eight-een.' Every time he got to the Swahili equivalent of the 'een' he rolled his head a trifle and shifted his hand a trifle — 'No advance on eight-een?'

No advance coming, he presently strolled away, leading his chattel by the hand, who strolled likewise, smiling.

There were several other girls and women near at hand whom I now observed with some attention.

They were decorated for the day in the latest fashions.

Their hair was newly frizzed, and worked up into innumerable little ridges from the forehead backwards, much resembling the drills left by a turnip-sowing machine on the land. Some boasted a trifling bead ornament or two in their ears and nostrils. Circles of blue-black khol surrounded each eye, giving it a horrible mask-like appearance. The chief ornament, however, was a heavy black line — apparently drawn with lampblack and oil — over one eyebrow, arched upwards, crossing the nose with a downward peak, and regaining the upward arch over the other eyebrow.

I heard one girl say something to her neighbour in reference to this ornament. The other girl smilingly replied, and put her face out to the first. She then, taking the end of her dress, carefully touched up the black line over the other's nose, which I now observed was somewhat irregular in curve. The transaction was a simple one and spoke many things to my inner consciousness . . . .

At another part of the market, sitting against a wall, were a group of what were pointed out to me as the most valuable female slaves. These wore dark veils thrown back from their foreheads, and were crowned, not unpicturesquely, with glittering spangles entwined in the folds of the veil. They wore more ornaments, and besides the black line, a broad band of filthy bright yellow paint invaded the upper part of the forehead and the lower part of the hair. I saw none of these put up for auction or sold: . . .

. . . . I did not see violence or rudeness of any kind; neither did I see coarseness or indecency. I did not see any preparation made for the employment of force: nor anything approaching to dissent from the proceedings on the part of the blacks. . . .

A few days after my first visit, I paid a second to the slave market, rather later in the evening. I was the more anxious to see it again, because some of the officers had described their seeing gross indecencies towards the women practised by intending buyers, and as I had seen no signs of anything of the kind, I was anxious to verify it.

The market was well on when we arrived. There were perhaps twenty auctioneers, each attending a separate group, and selling away as hard as possible. One of the officers counted over 300 slaves present, and it was clear several groups had only just been landed. My former friend with the bullet-head was dozily naming his eighteen or twenty dollars, as the case might be, altogether untouched by the excitement which seemed to govern some of his brethren or rivals.

One of these strongly attracted my notice. He was a young man, not altogether Arab in appearance, and with a not unpleasant cast of countenance. His counter was laid out with a choice selection of goods from the continent, and he was selling them, like a steam-engine.

His 'lot' appeared to be lately imported; they were all young boys and girls, some of them mere babies; and it was amongst them that the terribly painful part of the slave system was to be seen. I mean the miserable state, apparently of starvation, in which so many of these poor wretches are sometimes landed. The sight is simply horrible, and no amount of sophistry or sentiment will reconcile us to such a condition of things. Skeletons, with a diseased skin drawn tight over

them, eyeballs left hideously prominent by the falling away of the
surrounding flesh, chests shrunk and bent, joints unnaturally swelled
and horribly knotty by contrast with the wretched limbs between
them, voices dry and hard, and 'distantly near' like those of a
nightmare—these are the characteristics which mark too many of the
negroes when imported. All, however, are by no means so. I have
seen in the same batch, some of these skeletons, and others as plump
as possible. In this very group it was so. . . . .

My Arab auctioneer was working away at a boy when I first noticed
him. He had reached 16 dollars, but there seemed to be no advance. I
knew my friend to be selling, when I could only see his back, by the
steady periodical working thereof, caused by his vigorous decla-
mation.

'St—asher; St—asher; St—asher; St—asher; St—asher; St—asher,'
&c., thus the auctioneer, not looking at anyone in particular, or
seeming to attach any definite meaning to what he was doing. Only
the 'St—asher' came out of him like a jet of steam, and shook his
whole body and the body of the slave boy on whom his hand rested.

I addressed him through the interpreter,

'When did they land?'

Auctioneer. 'St—asher—two days ago—St—asher—St—asher,'
&c.

I. 'What will you let him go for?'

Auctioneer. (He never leaves off). 'St—asher—St—asher—twenty
dollars—St—asher,' &c.

No advance appearing on 'St—asher,' the boy was made to sit
down, and a little girl about six years old put up.

A wizened Arab with a quiet face and one eye, was amongst the
buyers. He looked at the child's little hands, and then stooped down
and spoke to her with a smiling face. The child smiled in return, and
I could not think that my wizened Arab would treat her *very* badly if
he bought her. She was soon worked up to the regulation 'St—asher,'
and two or three more bidders chimed in. The steam-engine worked
faster and faster; he had got to 'Sebba—t'asher; Sebba—t'asher;' and
in his hurry and work could only pluck at the dresses of probable
purchasers.

Wizen-face and the rest of the buyers are all very calm and do not
trouble their heads much about the matter, but the steam-engine will
certainly burst his boiler if it goes on much longer. Wizen-face,
impelled by a strong pull at his dress, advances a quarter of a dollar:
steam-engine plucks him again, with an advance of another quarter,
and goes on working madly. Wizen-face, however, is not inclined to
go further, and moves away. Steam-engine plucks him harder by the

dress, and, never leaving off his 'Sebba — t'asher — noos,' which is now the price, stoops down and gathers the child up in his arms, seeming to say, 'Come, take the little thing — she is only an armful.' Wizen-face will not buy, however, after all, and steam-engine blows off his steam, and sets the little girl on the ground preparatory to getting the steam up over a fresh article.

At this moment my attention was attracted in another direction, by hearing a sound as of a drowsy humble bee chanting in monotone. Passing through the crowd in the direction of the sound, I became aware of a string of some eight negro girls, standing in a row and facing me. These girls were decorated in the highest style of the fashion before described, but they each had, besides, a sort of mantle of blue muslin thrown lightly round their shoulders, which, it struck me, they were rather proud of. The humble bee from whom the buzzing proceeded was the auctioneer in charge of the sale of these girls. In appearance he looked like a benevolent edition of Mr. Fagin as we first make his acquaintance in the pages of 'Oliver Twist.' His beard was white and flowing, his nose hooked and prominent, and his eyes half closed and dreamy. He carried the regulation cane under his arm, was sauntering round and round his stock of goods, and making undecided changes in the 'sit' of the girls' attire with his disengaged hands. The drowsy buzzing which proceeded from his lips resolved itself into distinct sounds when I got near enough to analyse them.

The sounds were, 'Thelātha washerin wa noos;' 'thelātha washerin wa noos;' which, when separated into their proper words, became Swahili for 'twenty-three and a half,' twenty-three-and-a-half dollars being the upset price of each or any of the lot before me.

This humble bee differed from the other auctioneers, inasmuch as he did not seem to connect his buzzing chant with his stock-in-trade.

'Thelātha washerin wa noos, thelātha washerin wa noos, thelātha washerin wa noos;' it was more a song to pass away the time than an announcement of the upset price of his lots, as he sauntered backwards and forwards, now re-settling a fold of muslin which he had unsettled on his last passage, now patting the shoulder of this one, and now altering the position of the arm of that one, and never ceasing to chant the while.

I studied the faces of these girls very closely to try and detect what their feelings were on the subject, but it is almost as hopeless to penetrate the thoughts of a negro through his expression, as it is to get at those of a sheep by the same process. I could see neither pleasure, pain, nor any other active sentiment in their demeanour, or expression. Absence of thought, rather than presence of indifference, pervaded each countenance, and I could not help speculating whether it were more true that the thoughts which we, in our state of mental energy, would consider proper to such an occasion, were really present in these creatures' minds, but hidden from me by the negro conformation of features: or whether the thoughts were really absent. If I am to judge by what I have seen of the negro in his natural state, I must give it that the thought is absent.

I got my interpreter to ask one girl whether she liked it or no, but the only answer obtainable was that careless jerk out of the chin, which we associate with sulky indifference.

Passing from this group, I strolled to the wall against which were seated the superior slave women, whom I had noticed on a previous day. These were in charge of a jovial gentleman, with a sense of the comic in his demeanour, who took no apparent trouble to effect sales and whiled away the time whittling at a big stick. These slaves, I understood, had been some time in servitude, and came with characters from their former masters; hence their value. I could obtain no account of themselves or their feelings from these people. Stolid indifference as usual was marked in their faces and replies. The auctioneer seemed so taken up with the fun of the thing, that I could only get jokes out of him. By the way, this gentleman forcibly reminded me of Ali Baba, as I, in company with my children, had seen him at Covent Garden. Failing, therefore, to advance in my knowledge, I led the way from the market, which I did not afterwards re-visit.

I did not see, in open market, that revolting examination of the muscle of women for sale, which we know must go on. Such examinations were nominally private. The women being taken aside for the purpose.

And according to Livingstone, from his *Last Journals*, ed. Horace Waller, London 1874, Vol. 1., p. 7, in a report of 28 January 1866,

On visiting the slave-market I found about 300 slaves exposed for sale, the greater part of whom came from Lake Nyassa and the Shire River. Indeed one woman said that she had heard of our passing up L. Nyassa in a boat, but she did not see me: others came from Chipeta southwest of the Lake. All who have grown up seem ashamed at being hawked about for sale. The teeth are examined, the cloth lifted up to examine the lower limbs, and a stick is thrown for the slave to bring, and thus exhibit his paces. Some are dragged through the crowd by the hand, and the price called out incessantly: most of the purchasers are Northern Arabs and Persians.

And in a further report of 11 June 1866, Livingstone   stated

This is now almost the only spot in the world where 100 to 300 slaves are daily exposed for sale in open market. This disgraceful scene I several times personally witnessed, and the purchasers were Arabs or Persians, whose dhows lay anchored in the harbour, and these men were daily at their occupation examining the teeth, gait and limbs of the slaves, as openly as horse dealers engage in their business in England.

The scene of human beings penned and sold like cattle created nausea and disgust, and, according to Captain Colomb, in *Slave-Catching* pp. 392–3, it was dangerous to allow British seamen to go ashore at Zanzibar:

the blue jacket is impelled to make a clearance of the place, which he has more than once done on the spur of the moment.

Sir Bartle Frere described his visit to the Zanzibar slave market in 1873 in his report on his visit to East Africa.

On entering the market we passed by wooden sheds under which sat, on the left some half-caste Arabs, on the right, some half-clothed negroes. The market was comparatively empty when we arrived at half-past four in the afternoon, so we had a good opportunity of seeing the slaves who were already there. They were seated, in rows round the square, each batch sitting packed close together, and herded by an Arab or Negro (for the Negro seems to forget the miseries he once underwent — as a newly-captured slave, or, like a schoolboy bullied as a youngster, bullies again when able), who forced into position the luckless wretch who stretched his stiffening limbs beyond the limits allowed him.
We counted at that time ninety, of all ages, and of both sexes. Many wore a set and wearied look, many were fat and gay, while two young men and a boy alone confirmed, by their skeleton frames and looks of misery, the sensational tales often written of these markets. The impression left upon the mind at this time, was that the process of sales was not more debasing to the Negro than were the statute-hiring fairs of recent English times to the servant class of England. Most of the slaves were naked, some a clout round the waist of the men and a cloth thrown loosely over the women. I may say 'naked' for one can hardly consider as clothing what some held to be full-dress, viz. the scars and slashes on their faces, and the rings in their ears and noses. Some, however, of the women, chosen probably for some attraction which great doubtless to Zanzibarite eyes, were hardly appreciable by

Europeans, were gaudily dressed in coloured robes, with short-clipped hair; eyes and eyebrows painted black, and henna-dyed foreheads, while the rings and armlets they wore were heavy and large.

About 5 o'clock the frequenters of the market — the lounge of the true Zanzibarite, strolled quietly in, Arabs and half-caste Persians of the Guard in their long caps, and all armed with matchlock and dagger. At once the salesmen woke up, and all was bustle. And now came a cruel time. With a cruel knowledge of business, the sickliest and most wretched slaves were trotted out first, led round by the hand among the crowd and their price called out.

The price of one boy was seven dollars: he was stripped and examined by a connoiseur, his arms felt, his teeth examined, his eyes looked at, and finally he was rejected.

The examination of the women was still more disgusting. Bloated and henna-dyed old debauchees gloated over them, handled them from head to foot before a crowd of lookers-on, like a cowseller, or a horse-dealer, and finally when one was apparently satisfactory, buyer and seller and woman all retired behind the curtain of the shed to play out the final examination.

The prices we heard mentioned, varied from 67 dollars for a woman to 7 dollars for a boy whose case I mentioned. We saw no details actually effected, and were told that the presence of the Mission in Zanzibar had sensibly affected the commerce in slaves as well as in other ordinary articles of trade. This being the closing time, the market was not at its full height though there must have been at least 200 slaves there before we left.

No rudeness was shown to us by anyone, though I have been told that some officers of the squadron now here have been insulted and hissed by the Arabs.

The market place was a far more brutal and degrading sight than I ever saw in Egypt or Arabia, and no description could well do justice to its degradation."

SP LXI, 1873, No. 56, 29 May 1873

The role of the Sultan of Zanzibar and Oman in shielding the slave traders (and also the making of eunuchs), was commented on by Captain W. F. Owen, who carried out a survey of the East African coast in 1822-4. According to his Report to Admiralty; 8 iii, 24 (Adm. i 2269), *Narrative*, i, p. 342, the Sultan's 'power and purse' were upheld by this infamous commerce,

his soldiers and his servants are supplied by it, and the Red Sea and Persia and some parts of North India pay him immense sums annually for slaves to be cut for the seraglios and other faithful services for which those from the East Coast are held in the highest esteem.

Colonel Atkins Hamerton, first British Consul to Zanzibar, who arrived there in 1841, saw the full flood of the slave trade centred on Zanzibar. His reports on that trade were the first to stir the British government to take action against it. Shortly after his arrival in 1841, the *Zanzibar Archives*: Hamerton to Bombay Government, 13 July 1841, show that he reported

In no part of the world is the misery and human suffering the wretched slaves undergo while being brought here, and until they are sold, exceeded in any part of the Universe; they are in such a wretched state from starvation and disease that they are sometimes not considered worth landing, and are allowed to expire in the boats to save the duty of the dollar a head, and eaten by the dogs, none are buried.

These same Archives, Hamerton to Foreign Office, 4 October 1845, quote him as saying

I have seen fifty dead Africans, men and women, lying on the beach and the dogs tearing them to pieces as one sees the carrion eaten by the dogs in India.

Hamerton's reports on the slave trade at Zanzibar resulted in Lord Palmerston, British Foreign Secretary, writing to the Bombay Government in FO 84/647 Memorandum by Palmerston, 6 December 1846,

Captain Hamerton should take every opportunity of impressing upon these Arabs that the nations of Europe are destined to put an end to the African S.T., and that Great Britain is the main instrument in the Hands of Providence for the accomplishment of this purpose. That it is in vain for these Arabs to endeavour to resist the consummation of that which is written in the Book of Fate, and that they ought to bow to superior power, to leave off a pursuit which is doomed to annihilation, and a perseverance in which will only involve them in losses and other evils; and that they should hasten to betake themselves to the cultivation of their soil and to lawful and innocent commerce.

The first full-scale inquiry into the East African Slave Trade was carried out by the Select Committee of the House of Commons appointed in 1870. Its findings led directly to the negotiation of a treaty with the Sultan of Zanzibar to end the slave trade in his East African dominions and to close the slave market at Zanzibar.

THE SELECT COMMITTEE appointed to inquire into the whole question of the SLAVE-TRADE on the EAST COAST of AFRICA, into the increased and increasing amount of that Traffic, the Particulars of existing Treaties and Agreements with the Sultan of Zanzibar upon the subject, and the possibility of putting an end entirely to the Traffic in Slaves by Sea; — Have considered the matters to them referred, and have agreed to the following REPORT: —

"THAT the Slave-trade in negroes on the East Coast of Africa is now almost entirely confined to a trade between the dominions of Zanzibar on the one hand, and the coast of Arabia and Persia and the island of Madagascar on the other hand, the principal and by far the largest portion of the traffic being in the former direction. The dominions of Zanzibar extend along the eastern coast of Africa for about 350 miles, and lie between the Equator and ten degrees south latitude, and include the islands of Zanzibar, Pemba, and Momfia, the head-quarter of government being the island of Zanzibar, which lies opposite the centre of the coast-line, and about twenty-five miles from the mainland. The town of Zanzibar is rapidly growing in importance, as is evidenced by the progressive increase of imports at the Custom-house there, from 245,981l. in 1861-62, to 433,693l. in 1867-68, of which trade about one-half is in the hands of British-Indian subjects. It was reported in 1867 by General Rigby to be the chief market of the world for the supply of ivory, gum, and copal, and to have a rapidly increasing trade in hides, oils, seeds, and dyes, while sugar and cotton promise to figure largely amongst its future exports. The country in the interior of that part of Africa, and of which Zanzibar is the outlet, is said, according to the recent accounts of Livingstone and others, to be equal in resources to any part of India, and to be, as a rule, more healthy. Iron abounds in all directions, coal is to be found, and cotton can be grown to any extent.

"The negro slave in general passes through three stages ere he reaches his final destination.

"These are, (1) the land journey from his home to the coast (2) a short sea voyage to the island of Zanzibar, where is the open slave-market, and (3) the final sea passage from Zanzibar to Arabia, Persia, or Madagascar.

"From the evidence laid before the Committee it appears that the large majority of the slaves are now brought from the western side of the Lake Nyassa (a distance of nearly 500 miles from the coast) to Kilwa, which is the principal port of shipment for Zanzibar, and is near the southern limit of the Zanzibar dominons.

"Your Committee had before them extracts from despatches of Dr. Livingstone, addressed to the Earl of Clarendon, when her Majesty's

Secretary of State for Foreign Affairs, and his testimony as to the methods resorted to by the slave hunters; and the cruelties and horrors of the trade is fully supported by the evidence of witnesses who had travelled in the interior. This evidence is well summed up in the Report of the Committee on the East African Slave Trade, addressed to the Earl of Clarendon, a quotation from which is as follows: —

" 'The persons by whom this traffic is carried on are for the most part Arabs, subjects of the Sultan of Zanzibar. These slave dealers start for the interior, well armed, and provided with articles for the barter of slaves, such as beads and cotton cloth. On arriving at the scene of their operations, they incite and sometimes help the natives of one tribe to make war upon another. Their assistance almost invariably secures victory to the side which they support, and the captives become their property, either by right or by purchase, the price in the latter case being only a few yards of cotton cloth. In the course of these operations, thousands are killed, or die subsequently of their wounds or of starvation, villages are burnt, and the women and children carried away as slaves. The complete depopulation of the country between the coast and the present field of the slave dealers' operations attests the fearful character of these raids.

" 'Having by these and other means obtained a sufficient number of slaves to allow for the heavy losses on the road, the slave dealers start with them for the coast. The horrors attending this long journey have been fully described by Dr. Livingstone and others. The slaves are marched in gangs, the males with their necks yoked in heavy forked sticks, which at night are fastened to the ground, or lashed together so as to make escape impossible. The women and children are bound with thongs. Any attempt at escape or to untie their bonds, or any wavering or lagging on the journey, has but one punishment—immediate death. The sick are left behind, and the route of a slave caravan can be tracked by the dying and the dead. The Arabs only value these poor creatures at the price which they will fetch in the market, and if they are not likely to pay the cost of their conveyance they are got rid of. The result is, that a large number of the slaves die or are murdered on the journey, and the survivors arrive at their destination in a state of the greatest misery and emaciation.'

"From Kilwa the main body of the slaves are shipped to Zanzibar, but some are carried direct from Kilwa to the northern ports.

"At Zanzibar the slaves are sold either in open market or direct to the dealer, and they are then shipped in Arab dhows for Arabia and Persia; the numbers of each cargo vary from one or two slaves to between three and four hundred.

"The whole slave-trade by sea, whether for the supply of the Sultan's African dominions or the markets in Arabia and Persia, is carried on by Arabs from Muscat and other ports on the Arabian coast. They are not subjects of Zanzibar, but chiefly belong to tribes of roving and predatory habits.

"The sea passage exposes the slave to much suffering; and, in addition to the danger from overcrowding and insufficient food and water, the loss of life connected with the attempt to escape her Majesty's cruisers is very considerable, it being the practice to use any means to get rid of the slaves in order to escape condemnation, should the dhow be captured. Between Kilwa and Zanzibar a dhow lately lost a third of the slaves; there were ninety thrown overboard, dead or dying, many of them in a terribly emaciated state.

"The ready market found for the slave in Arabia and Persia, and the large profit upon the sale, are quite sufficient inducements for the continuance of the traffic.

"It seems impossible to arrive at an exact conclusion as to the actual number of slaves who leave the African coast in one year, but from the returns laid before the Committee an estimate may be formed. At the port of Kilwa is the Custom-house of the Sultan of Zanzibar, through which pass all slaves that are not smuggled, and there a tax is levied on all that pass the Custom-house.

"The following is a Return of the number of slaves exported through the Custom-house at Kilwa between 1862 and 1867, distinguishing those sent to Zanzibar from those shipped to other places: —

Year.	Zanzibar.	Elsewhere.
1862–63	13,000	5,500
1863–64	14,000	3,500
1864–65	13,821	3,000
1865–66	18,344	4,000
1866–67	17,538	4,500
	76,703	20,500
	20,500	

Total Exports from
Kilwa in five years   97,203

"From a despatch of Dr. Kirk, dated 1st February, 1870, it appears that 14,944 were exported from Kilwa in the year ending 23rd

August, 1869. But besides those passed through the Custom-house at Kilwa, numbers are exported from other places on the coast.

"Such is the extent to which the exportation of slaves takes place from the Zanzibar territory on the East Coast of Africa. It has also been shown that there the slave-trade still exists from the Portuguese territory to the island of Madagascar, and that slaves are still imported into Turkish ports in the Red Sea, General Rigby having recently seen fresh importations even in the civilized port of Suez. It must not, however, be thought that those who are taken captive, great as the numbers are, represent in any degree the total number of the sufferers from this iniquitous traffic. Such is the fearful loss of life resulting from this traffic, such the miseries which attend it, that, according to Dr Livingstone and others, not one in five, in some cases not one in ten, of the victims of the slave hunters ever reach the coast alive.   SP XII (I) 1871, No. 420, 4 August 1871

The slave trade based on Zanzibar was fed by the slave trade in the interior of East Africa which was channelled along caravan routes which debouched at Kilwa and Bagamoyo at the coast. Inland these routes branched out, spreading fan-like into the farthest reaches of the eastern Congo, Uganda and the Nyasa area. Along these routes slaves were drawn eastward from a vast area. There was no longer an outlet for slaves on the west coast; only on the eastern and northeastern side of the continent was there egress.

First-hand accounts of the condition of slaves on the long trek to the coast are not in agreement as to their treatment. Burton and Stanley attribute an almost hearty enjoyment and cheerfulness on the part of the slaves. Livingstone, Waller, Hutley and Elton, on the other hand, were appalled at what they saw in the way of brutality, crudeness and filth in which the slaves were immured. They could not find words strong enough to express their abhorrence of the slavers.

Africans were also involved in the slave trade of the interior, as the following accounts of the Ngoni, Masai, Wanyamwezi, and Manyuema will show. Sir Harry Johnston averred that the Manyuema must have had Arab blood in their veins, so addicted were they to slaving.

As to the wastage in slaves in the slave caravans on their way to the coast, Horace Waller commented, in Evidence before Select Committee 1870–1,

It is like sending up a large block of ice to London in the hot weather; you know that a certain amount will melt away before it reaches you in the country as it travels down; but that which remains will be quite sufficient for your wants.

The long-held view that ivory from the interior was carried to the coast by freshly captured slaves has little evidence to support it, according to Acting-Consul Seward to the Chief Secretary, Bombay Government.

The large and valuable tusks were not carried by the slaves, they were borne along by the porters or servants of the Arabs: the small tusks easily carried in hand were carried by a few of the slaves.

SP LXIV, 1867-8, No. 115, 25 October, 1866.

Richard Burton, who journeyed along the great slave route to Lake Tanganyika in 1860, states in *The Lake Regions of Central Africa*, Vol. II, London, 1860, p. 367, that

Justice requires the confession that the horrors of slave-driving rarely meets the eye in East Africa.

And H. M. Stanley, on his way to Ujiji in 1871, records in *How I found Livingstone*, London, 1890, p. 91, that he

met one of those sights common in this part of the world, to wit a chain slave-gang, bound east. The slaves did not appear to be in any way down-hearted, on the contrary, they seemed imbued with the philosophic jollity of the jolly servant of Martin Chuzzlewit. Were it not for their chains, it would have been difficult to discover master from slave: the physiognomic traits were alike —the mild benignity with which we were regarded was equally visible on all faces.

In 1865, Livingstone's *'Narrative of an Expedition to the Zambezi and its Tributaries'* appeared, in which the desolation and horror caused by the slavers in the Nyassa region was described. In the valley of the Shire, Livingstone met

The slave party, a long line of manacled men, women, and children came wending their way round the hill and into the valley, on the side of which the village stood. The black drivers, armed with muskets, and bedecked with various articles of finery, marched jauntily in front, middle, and rear of the line, some of them blowing exulting notes out of long tin horns. They seemed to feel that they were doing a very noble thing, and might proudly march with an air of triumph. But the instant the fellows caught a glimpse of the English, they darted off like mad into the forest; so fast, indeed, that we caught but a glimpse of their red caps and the soles of their feet. The chief of the party alone remained, and he, from being in front, had his hand tightly grasped by a Makololo. He proved to be a well known slave of the late commandant at Tette, and for some time our own attendant while there. On asking him how he obtained these captives, he replied he had bought them; but our inquiring of the people themselves, all save four said they had been captured in war. While this enquiry was going on, he bolted too.

The captives knelt down, and in their way of expressing thanks, clapped their hands with great energy. They were thus left entirely on our hands, and knives were soon busy at work cutting the women and children loose. It was more difficult to cut the men adrift, as each had his neck in the fork of a stout stick, six or seven feet long, and kept in by an iron rod which was riveted at both ends across the throat. With a saw, luckily in the Bishop's baggage, one by one the men were sawn out into freedom. The women, on being told to take the meal they were carrying, and cook breakfast for themselves and the children, seemed to consider the news too good to be true; but, after a little coaxing, went at it with alacrity, and made a capital fire by which to boil their pots, with the slave sticks and bonds, their old acquaintances through many a sad night and weary day. Many were mere children, about five years of age and under. One little boy, with the simplicity of childhood, said to our men, 'The others tied and starved us; you cut our ropes and tell us to eat. What sort of people are you? Where did you come from?' Two of the women had been shot the day before, for attempting to untie the thongs. This, the rest were told, was to prevent them attempting to escape. One woman had her infant's brains knocked out because she could not carry her load and it; and a man was despatched with an axe, because he had broken down with fatigue.

Livingstone went on to state that

It is our deliberate opinion, from what we know and have seen, that not one-fifth of the victims of the slave-trade ever become slaves. Taking the Shire valley as an average, we should say, not even one-tenth arrive at their destination.

The following description of a slave-gang is taken from the *Anti-Slavery Reporter*, Vol. 12, No. 5, 1 April 1873.

A SLAVE-GANG IN EAST AFRICA ON ITS WAY TO THE COAST.

I will just give you a description of the first slave-gang that we came across. It was on our second day's march into the hills. We breakfasted one morning at a village about ten o'clock, and, after getting a bath in the stream and so forth, we were beginning to write up our notes of the previous day and do whatever was necessary, for we could not march very far the second day, having been so long on board ship, when I heard a horn blowing, and I saw some talk going on among the natives. Livingstone had, at that time, a number of men called Makalolo with him. They had travelled with him from the interior of Africa, and well knew his hatred of the slave-trade, and there was, therefore, a little commotion among them, for they thought the fact of eight or ten Englishmen being there, and a gang of slaves coming down, was likely to lead to some interference. I went to Livingstone and told him that I had heard there was a slave-gang coming down. He said "I have also heard it this minute." What could be done in the matter? We were resolved that this slave-gang should not pass on. Well, in less time than I take to talk about it, these unfortunate creatures—eighty-four of them—wended their way into the village where we were. Some of them, the eldest, were women from 20 to 22 years of age, and there were youths from 18 to 19, but the large majority was made up of boys and girls from 7 years to 14 or 15 years of age. A more terrible scene than these men, women and children, I do not think I ever came across. To say that they were emaciated would not give you an idea of what human beings can undergo under certain circumstances. To imagine that any poor creatures could march on for five or six weeks, as these poor people had been doing, in the utter state of torture in which they were seems almost incredible. I believe the physique of the white man could never have endured it. Each of them had his neck in a large forked stick, weighing from thirty to forty pounds, and five or six feet long, cut with a fork at the end of it where the branches of a tree spread out. Each man's neck was placed in this, and an iron pin was run through. The pin was as thick as one's little finger, and was generally put in red hot to burn the wood, and then twisted round with a powerful pair of tongs, so that it was utterly impossible for him ever to get it off. The next man behind him had his stick twisted round in front, and the two were lashed together, so that the stick of one protruded behind, and the other had his in front of his throat, and the two were obliged to march in Indian file for five or six weeks together. The women were tethered with bark thongs, which are of all things the most cruel to be tied with. Of course they are soft and supple when first stripped of the trees, but a few hours in the sun make them about as hard as the iron round packing-cases. The little children were fastened by thongs to their mothers, because the most valuable slave is a young mother who has a child just old enough to walk after her. So this miserable gang of human beings came into the village one after another, the picture of despair. One man whom I saw limping along, had been struck by a fish spear in the heel some two months before. When I tell you that the heel was swollen up to the size of a cocoanut, and was discharging in a most horrible way—and under my treatment for two months never healed up till a great part of the bone came away—you may imagine what his sufferings had been. But these slaves had been bought so cheaply that it was worth while to see how long they could endure. Well, Livingstone and those who were with him dashed at the slave-hunters and seized them. There was no recourse to firearms or anything of that kind, because several of these men recognised Livingstone as having been in the Portuguese settlement of Tette. One of them was the servant of the Governor of Tette — who, I have no doubt, in his dispatches to the Home country, appears as philanthropic as Livingstone, and as carrying out all those pretty commands sent from Portugal to the different Portuguese settlements, but he was the greatest slaver of the lot; and we knew it then, and could prove it. The first thing, then, was what to do with these poor people. The first act of an English saw in that part of the world was to cut off one of those sticks from one of the poor fellows, and in less than half an hour we were able, partly through interpreters and partly through our looks and deeds, to show to these poor people that they were free. We then took all their sticks and bonds, and made them into a large heap, and set fire to them. We took from the slavers all the calico they had — for that is the currency of the country. We clothed them with this calico, which was intended to buy fresh slaves with, and we gave them all the food. This, however, is but the pleasing side of the subject, for on the next day we resumed our march, and then it was that I began to learn something of the slave-trade in its true horrors. As we passed along the path which these slaves had travelled a few hours before, I heard muttering and whispering, and noticed a sad look on their faces. Then I was shown a spot in the bushes where a poor woman the day before, unable to keep on the march, and likely to hinder it, was cut down by the axe of one of these slave-drivers; her bonds were then cut in two, and her body cast into the bushes. We went on further and were shown a place where a child lay. It had been recently born, and its mother was unable to carry it on from debility and exhaustion; so the slave-trader had taken this little infant by its feet and dashed its brains out against one of the trees, and thrown it in there. — *Extract of the Rev. Horace Waller's speech at the Friends' Meeting House, Bishopsgate Street, London.*

The extent of the land slave trade that sprang up along the East African coast following the 1873 treaty was reported on by Vice-Consul Elton to Captain Prideaux, during the course of a journey from Dar es Salaam southwards to Kilwa in the latter half of 1873.

The plain truth is, and there can be no disputing facts, that a brisker Slave Trade has seldom been known than the one carried on from Kilwa *via* the Kisiju Road by the scoundrels who hold it in their power, and who will continue to use it until put down by a strong hand, Burgash's orders being totally disregarded, except absolutely on the seacoast villages and towns, and even there only respected when they do not run counter to local and private interests.

"According to Abd-el-Kader, we must have passed 700 slaves on the 22nd — 350 in the first caravan; 150 in the second, which turned off the road for us and we missed, but which Vissonji Nersi an hour later met; and 200 in the third, the one met at Mangatani.

"On the 23rd, 200 passed through Kisiju, and a caravan of 300 turned off yesterday, 25th, hearing we were in the town, and slept in an adjoining village; making in all a total of 1,200 slaves; to which must be added the caravan missed at Kingonga on the 21st (said to be a small one of 80), and one week's traffic on the Kisiju Road represents a grand total of 1,280 slaves marched up from Kilwa for sale at the northern ports and Pemba. . . . .

One gang of lads and women chained together with iron neck rings was in a horrible state, their lower extremities coated with dry mud and their own excrement and torn with thorns, their bodies mere frameworks and their skelton limbs tightly stretched over with wrinkled parchment-like skin. One wretched woman had been flung against a tree for slipping her rope, and came screaming up to us for protection, with one eye half out, and the side of her face and bosom streaming with blood.

SP LXII 1874, No. 2, 26 December 1873

Among slave children there was a deep-rooted aversion to recalling the scenes of earlier life, and Sir Bartle Frere's report of 29 May 1873 says,

whenever the child could be got to recount the history of its capture, the tale was almost invariably one of surprise, kidnapping and generally of murder, always of indescribable suffering on the way down to the coast and on the dhow voyage.

Mr W. Hutley, of the London Missionary Society, who resided in Central and Eastern Africa for five years, described in an account in *The Times* of 30 May 1882 the slave trading activities of two tribes; the Wanyamwezi (in what is present-day central Tanzania) and the Manyuema (eastern Congo).

THE WANYAMWEZI.

The principal tribe of the interior is that of the Wanyamwezi. It is the largest in population and the greatest in influence. They are in four great divisions, each of which has a dialect of its own, and sometimes two or three. Each of these divisions has its own chief, who has in nearly all cases acquired great fame and influence as a warrior and leader. Their superiority among other tribes may be placed to their aptitude and ability for travel and colonization, also their keenness as traders. It is among these people, at Unyanyembe, that the Arabs have their chief depot for ivory and slaves, and where, as a consequence, they congregate in their greatest numbers. From men belonging to this tribe they derive their chief supply of human kind. Either these Wanyamwezi go out upon their own responsibility or are sent out in the employ of these Arabs for the purpose of trade. From out of their midst there is also a constant supply of slaves, which are captured in their wars upon each other. They also keep many of these slaves for themselves, and if they cannot obtain them as prisoners of war they will buy them. The price of a slave varies very much among them, but the price paid for a "green" or raw slave is generally a good Tower musket. These Tower muskets are the great articles of barter used by the Arabs among the Wanyamwezi.

Among these Wanyamwezi the slave is treated, as a rule, with the same feeling that we treat an animal, and although some of these slaves feel keenly the separation from their friends, yet they rarely attempt to run away. It is very difficult to get at statistics with regard to these slaves, but I am understating the mark when I say that one-fourth of the population of Unyamwezi are slaves.

The chief supply of slaves is now obtained in Manyuema, where the Arabs have also a depot. Most of the Arabs in the interior have their agents or partners there, through whom the supply of slaves and ivory is kept up. The mortality among these slaves is very great. I was informed at Ujiji of one Arab, Syeb-bin-Habib, who brought some 300 slaves with him from Manyuema; but of these 300, not more than 50 reached Unyanyembe. This was an excessively high mortality, but from my own experience of various caravans, the death-rate would be quite 50 per cent. of those who are slaves. This high rate is only so maintained during the journey. Every year large caravans come from Manyuema with supplies of slaves for the markets of Ujiji and Unyanyembe, from whence many of them find their way to the coast. It is difficult to say exactly how many do come in this way, but from all that I gathered and saw upon the spot during the years 1878 to 1881, at least, notwithstanding the excessive mortality, 1,000 slaves reached each of these two markets annually. In Ujiji these Manyuema slaves are in great demand. They are bought from the Arab traders in ones and twos by the natives, and are then retained as household slaves, or are taken into the neighbouring country of Uhha, and there exchanged for oxen, the value of a man slave and an ox being equal. Whenever a large caravan leaves Manyuema, it is always accompanied by numbers of free natives who have one or two slaves of their own for sale, who they will engage to the Arabs to carry the ivory. They seem to have imbibed a passion for firearms, which are now being imported into their country in hundreds, and the idea they have of them is to supply themselves with the means of maintaining the Slave-trade.

Scenes of savagery wrought by one tribe over another are frequently described. In the Mbe country of what is now Kenya, Captain Dundas, RN, witnessed a scene following a Masai raid. His account appears in the *Scottish Geographical Magazine* of March 1893.

On our return through the Mbe country, a most harrowing sight presented itself: what only a few days before were prosperous villages, standing amid fields of grain, were now smoking ruins; bodies of old men, women and children, half-burnt lay in all directions; here and there might be seen a few solitary individuals, sitting with their head buried in their hands, hardly noticing the passing caravan, and apparently in the lowest depths of misery and despair. On questioning several of these unhappy beings, I was informed that the Masai had unexpectedly arrived one morning at dawn, spearing and burning all before them and carrying off some 250 women, and large herds of cattle. Only a few of the unfortunate people had escaped by flying to the mountains.

And in an account in the *Free Church Monthly* of November 1892, one of the garrison at Karonga's, on the northwest corner of Lake Nyasa, stated

Last Friday night, 18th November, the Angoni came down to the Lake in great numbers, and attacked the village at Kayuni. They entered the village silently, and each warrior took up his position at the door of a hut, and ordered the inmates to come forth. Every man and boy was speared as he emerged and every woman captured. News of this disaster soon reached the three white men stationed at Karonga's in the employ of the Lakes Company. One of their number set out immediately with fifty guns to re-capture the women, who, to the number of 200 or 300 were being carried off. In the afternoon they met the Angoni and opened fire. Taken by surprise, the raiders made off, but, not being able to carry both the booty and the women, they began immediately to spear the latter. A horrible scene then ensued. In half an hour they were beaten off and the women rescued. I was at the scene of the disaster three days after, and counted forty-seven wounded. The others had either died or been carried off by friends. One man had fifteen spear-wounds; a child of two years had seven. What impressed me most was the number of young girls and children (even on the breast) who were speared. The poor creatures were afraid to go to their village, and were living in the reeds lining the lake shore. As far as can be ascertained, the following is the list of dead: Men 29; women about 100; girls 32; boys 16; Angoni about 30."

THE ARAB, ISLAM AND SLAVERY

The slave once in possession of his Muslim master, Arab or Swahili, was kindly treated. The possession of a slave meant the entry into a new relationship, master versus slave; it meant the fulfillment for the Arab of an aspiration. The *Zanzibar Archives* of 2 February 1842 show that according to Hamerton, British consul at Zanzibar, to the Bombay Government, slaves were essential,

as a sign of wealth and respectability, a freed man Mussulman never dreams of doing any sort of labour but lives off his slaves.

And Captain Cornish-Bowden, in 1865, stated:

The whole seaboard population is Mahommedan; they think slavery a divine right, cannot undersand our views, and ask why we, a great nation, steal their slaves, when we can buy them so cheaply.

SP LXXV, 1866, No. 97, 30 June 1865.

In the Transactions of the Bombay Geographical Series, vi, 1844, pp. 43-4, Captain Smee, who visited Zanzibar in 1811, stated that

The Arabs are justly famed for the mild treatment of their slaves. They are not overworked, are allowed to live on their master's estate and grow their own food, and seem fairly happy and contented.

And according to Captain W. F. Owen's *Narrative*, Vol. II, p. 155,

The condition of the slaves belonging to the Arabs of Mombas is highly creditable to their humanity; they cannot always be distinguished from their masters, as they are allowed to imitate them in dress and in other particulars.

This kindliness on the part of the Arabs towards their slaves extended into the Middle East. Even in the present century Wilfred Thesiger in *Arabian Sands*, New York, 1959, p. 64, notes how the Emir of Salala greeted as an equal an old black slave, and at dinner served him with his own hands.

And a special tribute to the Arabs for their charity and kindly treatment of their slaves came from Sir Lloyd (General) Mathews who commanded the Sultan of Zanzibar's forces in the later nineteenth century and had ample time and opportunity to ruminate on the matter. To Sir Arthur Hardinge, British Consul-General at Zanzibar, he wrote,

From my own observation as regards charity, the Mahommedans, in their quiet unostentatious manner of giving relief, practically not letting their left hand know what the right hand has done, teach us Christians and our professional philanthropists a good lesson. An earthly recompense is not looked for by them. The poorest man can enter a Mahommedan house and ask for a meal; he will not be sent away fasting, and will generally receive something for the following day. This is absolutely true, and shows that Mahomedans are not the monsters of cruelty they are painted by those who aim at publicity by preaching a 'jehad' against the Arabs from their comfortable armchairs in England. There are, of course, exceptions; I do not say all are good, but even the worst treat their slaves far better than many householders at home treat their so-called 'Slaveys', or husbands their wives in the East End of London.

To my mind, the above shows that the gradual freeing of slaves by the Decree abolishing the legal status of slavery is a very wise method. There is no fear of slaves being ill-treated now they have the same rights in Courts of law as their masters; they are paid for their labour, and can obtain their freedom when they please. A gradual emancipation teaches them their position by giving them time to judge for themselves, to think of their future, and act when it pleases them, instead of leaving their masters without thought, becoming vagrants, and pauperized.   FOCP 7401/41, 17 March 1899

From Mr (later Sir) Arthur Hardinge, on 11 May 1895, in *Africa* No. 7, C-8275, 1896,

The testimony of every European resident in Zanzibar would, however, I believe, be that the Slave population is, on the whole, contented, and materially a good deal better off in relation to its wants than the labouring classes in most countries of Europe, so that the necessity of abolition is only urgent from a moral point of view, if the theoretical injustice and inequality of the system of slavery, an injustice not felt by the Slaves themselves, since it is in accordance with their own religious and social conceptions, is to outweigh every other interest . . . .
Critics at home if they wish to understand Mohammedan domestic slavery and family life must banish from their minds all the associations of 'Uncle Tom's Cabin' and similar works, and transport themselves in imagination to the familiar scenes of the Bible.

One last report from Hardinge says,

A curious instance came before me recently, as showing how

completely the system of slavery has permeated the whole life of this people. A slave who had slaves of his own, complained to me that his master wished to take them away from him because he had not given him enough labour and I found on further inquiry that the master in question was himself a slave of the well-known Tanganyika Arab — Mohomed-bin Khalifan, or Rumaliza.

FOCP 6717/184, 27 April 1895

THE KORAN AND SLAVERY

The following extract by Mr John Scott, Judge in the Egyptian Court of Appeal, appeared in the *Anti-Slavery Reporter,* Vol. II, Fourth Series, May 1882.

Does the Koran after all sanction this modern form of Slavery? I am inclined to think that the Mahomedan authorities who were consulted in 1877 opined that it did not, and I believe they were right. I have searched the Koran from end to end, and I find that the retention of captives taken in war and not ransomed is the only form of Slavery sanctioned by Mahomet (Koran, ch. 47, v. 4. and 5). The Prophet would have shrunk with horror from the present system, under which men, women, and children are hurried from their tropical homes, dragged in chains, driven with whips down to the sea coast, or to the river, or to the desert tracks, and finally a miserable remnant of them sold in the market at Cairo or Constantinople. "Show kindness to your slaves." (ch. 4, 40), says Mahomet, and again "Alms should buy the freedom of slaves." (Ch. 9, 60.) But the great doctrine of emancipation itself is preached in one remarkable injunction which might well be printed in letters of gold on the walls of every Mahomemedan mosque as a preamble to an Arabic translation of the Slave-trade convention. It runs thus:-

"If any one of your slaves asks from you his freedom give it him if you judge him worthy of it; grant them a little of the goods which God has granted you." (Ch. 24, v. 33).

The following outline of the religious laws governing slavery, addressed to the Earl of Kimberley by Arthur Hardinge, appeared in *Africa* No. 6 C-7707, 26 February 1895.

In Zanzibar as in other Moslem countries the institution of slavery rests upon the "Sheria," or religious law, which is here, unlike that of Turkey and Egypt, the secular and municipal law also. This law has been modified in practice (1) by local custom, and (2) by the arbitrary Edicts of despotic Rulers issued under foreign pressure, and which, whilst condemned by native public opinion as illegal and contrary to the faith, and evaded whenever possible, have been enforced from time to time in a greater or less degree by the physical power of the infidel.

The following are the legal disabilities which the Mahommedan religion and law (and the two are in Zanzibar, save for the exceptions mentioned above, identical) impose upon the slave: —

(*a*.) He cannot own, or acquire, or dispose of private property without the permission of his master.

(*b*.) He cannot give evidence in a Court of Justice, nor, without his master's sanction, take an oath.

(*c*.) He cannot, without the sanction of his master, contract a legal marriage, nor, according to most of the doctors, even with the permission of his master, have more than two wives at the same time.

(*d*.) He cannot sue his master before a Court of law, unless severely ill-treated by the latter. In case of such ill-treatment the Cadi may and ought to warn the master that if the complaint is repeated, and proved genuine, he will forfeit his slave. Should the slave sue his master a second time, and the charge of cruelty be established, the Cadi may order the slave to be valued and sold, and the purchase-money to be paid to the master.

(*e*.) He cannot sue any other person, whether free or slave, without his master's consent; with it, he is free to do so.

(*f*.) He cannot, without his master's permission, engage in trade, undertake a journey, or even make the pilgrimage to Mecca, nor in general claim any legal or civil right, except through and with his master's sanction.

(*g*.) There is no legal limitation to his master's power of punishing him, and, theoretically, I believe that he might put him to death without himself being held guilty of murder, or of any more serious offence than cruelty.

The principle of the Mosaic law which made it penal to scourge a slave to death, if he died under the lash, but not if he survived it one day (Exodus xxi, 20), on the ground that the slave was "his master's money," and his loss a sufficient penalty in itself, would appear to have been followed to a still harsher and more logical conclusion by the Mahommedan jurists; but, in practice, I imagine that in most Moslem countries, even without European pressure, the equity of the Ruler would be allowed to correct the injustice of the law, and that the severe, though not the capital, punishment of a master proved to have recklessly killed his slave would commend itself to the popular sense of right.*

* In Zanzibar usage, sanctioned by the Cadis, obliged the master to pay to the 'beitel-mal', or public treasury, a sum equal to half the blood-money

A master may imprison his slave for a short term, and may give him nineteen strokes at a time as a punishment for an offence without being held guilty, by the usage of Zanzibar, of cruelty. To beat him without cause, or to inflict a really cruel beating with cause, would justify the Cadi, if complained to by the slave, and if the cruelty had been repeated twice, in ordering his master to sell him. The Ibadhis, I believe, allow the punishments which a master may inflict without committing cruelty to be somewhat more severe than is the case among the Sunnis.

(h.) Save the general prohibition described above of ill-treatment or cruelty, there is no legal limitation to the amount or nature of the work which a master may impose on his slave, whether the latter be a man, woman, or a child.

These disabilities are mitigated as follows: (a) by custom, (b) by the arbitrary power of the Sultan.

(a.) In practice slaves do hold property of their own, and are allowed by their masters to dispose of it. It is quite a common thing for a slave to have slaves of his own, and to treat the produce of their labour as his personal property. In practice, moreover, the slave is always allowed to labour two days in the week (Thursday and Friday), or at least one day (Friday) for himself and his family alone, and what he earns on those days is regarded by local custom as exclusively his. He is also permitted to retain a small portion of what he earns while working for his master, and once every six months he is entitled to new clothing (one shirt or white cotton gown for a man, two pieces of cloth for a woman). If his master gives him neither board, lodging, nor clothing beyond the regular half-yearly allowance mentioned above he is entitled to half his earnings, or (taking an average) 2 dollars or 2½ dollars a month. Should his master refuse it him he can be summoned on the slave's complaint by the Cadi, and ordered to pay the slave, and, in the event of his persisting in his refusal, he can be imprisoned, not, however, be it noted, for harshness to his slave, but for contempt of the Cadi's order. If the slave gets no pay he is entitled to a portion of a room, a bed, and any

---

which would have been required for the murder of a freeman, and to be kept in prison at the Sultan's pleasure; but cases of the killing of a slave by his owner were, I believe, of rare occurrence. Barghash once imprisoned a master for six months for castrating two slaves who had ravished his daughter, on the ground that, although their crime deserved severe punishment, it was for the Sultan, not the master, to inflict it. If a slave is killed by a freeman, not his master, the law obliges the latter to pay the blood-money to the owner, though some jurists say that the owner may refuse to take it, and may insist on the killer being put to death. The killing of one slave by another slave is a capital offence.

food left over from his master's meals or cooked by the slaves of the house, or, in place of food, to 2 annas a day out of his earnings. If he is invalided, custom obliges the master to provide for him. Only last week I freed a slave on the ground of cruelty on the part of his master, who had turned him adrift when unfit, on account of a bad leg, to work, and who then, as soon as his leg was healed, seized and forced him to return to labour. All these relaxations and indulgences are, strictly speaking, conventional rather than legal, but they have become so stereotyped by custom that the Courts consider themselves justified in regarding a refusal to grant them as technically equivalent to cruelty. I have always myself so considered them, and have several times on that ground given their freedom to slaves who complained that they had been without reason withheld.

(b.) The Sultan, by the exercise of his authority as Hakim, or temporal Ruler, prohibits the sale of slaves. In a case of "cruelty," therefore, the slave has to be liberated without the compensation which the letter of the law gives the master. This procedure being, however, contrary to the Sheria, a Cadi would not apply it himself, but would send the parties to His Highness.

I will now proceed to describe the means by which a slave can acquire his freedom (a) by the law and (b) by the usage and positive Edicts of the Sultans, which have modified it.

According to Mahommedan law, no authority whatever, except his master, can free a slave.

There are, so far as I know, only three exceptions to this rule: —*

1. After the death of a master, two witnesses, being men of good repute, declare before a Cadi that they heard the deceased verbally pronounce the slave to be free. The Cadi can then free him without reference to the claims of the heirs. Some of the jurists of the Ibadhi sect, to which the Sultan and the Zanzibar Arabs, as distinct from the Swahilis, belong, doubt the lawfulness of such manumission on mere hearsay evidence. I may observe, indeed, that the general doctrines of this sect are much less favourable to the rights of the slave than those of orthodox Mahommedanism with which they are occasionally in

---

* Throughout this despatch, in speaking of Mahommedan law I must be understood, where the contrary is not specified, to mean orthodox Sunni law, like that of Turkey and Egypt. The vast majority of the inhabitants of Zanzibar, outside the dominant class, are Sunnis of the Shafei sect. The slaves, though circumcised and nominal Moslems are practically, many of them, little better than heathens; but even in Ibadhi households they are reckoned as Sunnis, being usually admitted to Islam by a Sunni fellow slave, and thus following the sect of their spiritual father. The Ibadhis, who took on their own sect as an Arab and aristocratical one, rather scorn, I fancy, to admit slaves to it.

conflict on points of the law of slavery, and that emancipation among the Ibadhis is a good deal rarer than among Sunnis.

2. A concubine who bears her master a child, if not actually freed by him on its birth, becomes *ipso facto* a free woman at his death, and cannot even during his lifetime be sold. This form of emancipation, which is known to the law as "istilad," is, of course, dependent on the master recognizing the child, which in most Mahommedan countries he is not strictly bound to do, even though he may believe it to be his; in Zanzibar he usually so recognizes it, but the "mustallida," or "umm-el-walad," as the mother is called, does not necessarily acquire absolute freedom till after the master's death. The latter cannot sell her, but he may lawfully continue, without marrying, to cohabit with her so long as she is a slave, unless he should give her in marriage to another man, in which case she must be divorced before he can again have intercourse with her. I should add that a slave concubine, not being an "umm-el-walad," cannot, if married with her master's consent, and not divorced by her husband, be sold, but her master may compel her to work for him. Her children, even if her husband is a freeman, are slaves, and their master may make them work for him, but, like their mother, they cannot be sold. According to the Ibadhis, though the master cannot sell a concubine by whom he has had a child, her immunity ceases at his death, and she can be offered for sale by his children born of wives who inherit her as their property, and who can usually insure her being bought by her own children, the latter, though not heirs, being free. This cruel practice was prohibited for a time by Seyyid Barghash, who was himself the son of a slave, but his prohibition had, of course, no legal force.

3. A person committing certain specified sins, such as breaking the Ramadan fast, killing another Mahommedan accidentally and unintentionally ("katl-el-hatta"), and divorcing his wife by "zihar" (*e.g.*, by saying to her, "thou art to me as my mother's or sister's back," for which he must perform "kafarah," or expiation, before resuming conjugal rights), may be ordered by the Cadi to manumit a slave, or to feed a certain number of poor persons as "tahrir," or atonement.

Exclusive of these peculiar modes of emancipation, there are three forms by which a master can manumit: —

1. "Atak," the verbal grant of immediate and unconditional freedom.

2. "Tadbir," a promise of freedom contingent on the master's death, and revocable by him at pleasure at any time before it, but otherwise conferring freedom immediately the master dies, not only

on the slave himself, but on all his children born subsequent to the promise; and

3. "Kitabah," a written agreement to free the slave on certain conditions such as the payment in instalments of a ransom, pending the completion of which the slave, under the title of "mukaltib," enjoys a certain amount of personal freedom, but cannot by himself perform any valid legal or civil act.

Of these three modes of manumission, I believe "tadbir" to be the commonest in Zanzibar at present; "kitabah" is, I am told, a good deal rarer.

It should be remembered, in this connection, that the emancipation of slaves is a very meritorious act in the eyes of the Mahommedan religion, and that it has always been common for devout Moslems to purchase them with this specific object, a bequest of money for this purpose by will (called "curbah," or a pious gift) being considered peculiarly commendable.

It is a tradition that the Prophet once exclaimed: 'Whosoever shall free a Moslem slave God will free every member of his body, limb by limb, from the fire of hell."

The emancipation by a stranger, such as a British Consul or other authority, of slaves purchased with this religious intention, is therefore strongly resented by their owners, as depriving them of the merits of their contemplated act, and defrauding them, so to speak, of an investment in the world to come.

To sum up, whilst the Mahommedan law generally encourages emancipation, it requires, with a very few exceptions, that it should be the master's own free and spontaneous act.

At Zanzibar, however, the principles described above, although theoretically immutable, have been undermined by the operation of modern non-Mahommedan legislation, such as the Treaty between Seyyid Barghash and Her Majesty forbidding the introduction of any slaves by sea, the Decree of Seyyid Khalifa giving freedom to all slaves entering his territory after a certain date, that of Seyyid Ali prohibiting the sale and purchase of slaves, or their acquisition by any means save direct inheritance, and the Articles in the Brussels Act permitting and directing emancipation by a variety of authorities unknown to the Sacred law.

Thus both the Sultan and I myself habitually free slaves in the exercise, so to speak, of our prerogative. His Highness, I believe, keeps within the letter of the law, by ordering the master in every case to free the slave himself, thus maintaining the fiction of a voluntary act, since no Arab or Swahili Hampden would ever be found to insist on legal rights, in the face of a Royal command. I of course simply grant papers of freedom, without regard either to the letter or to the spirit of the law.

It is indeed very doubtful whether emancipation granted, even by a master, under compulsion, could be regarded as legally valid in the native Courts. They would certainly not recognize emancipation by myself or the Brussels Act, and, as far as they dared (and they are very timid when dealing with the Sultan), they would, if appealed to, hardly be able to help pronouncing it invalid.

Suppose, for instance, a slave freed by me contrary to the Sheria were to bring an action against his former master, and that the latter were to plead that the emancipation was illegal, and that the plaintiff was still a slave, and therefore could not sue him, the Cadi would, according to strict law, be obliged to dismiss the case, and would probably do so, if he fancied it would go no further; but if the slave were shrewd enough to threaten him with the Sultan's anger for ignoring one of his Decrees, he would most likely discover some pretext for referring the dispute to His Highness, and thus shifting on to the shoulders of the latter the responsibility of breaking the Sacred Law. One convenient and rather interesting loophole for the Cadis of the Ibadhi sect is the doctrine of "takiah," or pious hypocrisy, which permits a man to commit an action forbidden by God, if necessary, to save himself, so long as he abhors it in his heart. Thus the chief Ibadhi Cadi here once told me, in reply to a question which I had put to him, that it would not be sinful for him to eat pork, if commanded by a tyrant to do so on pain of punishment, and when I cited to him the examples of Daniel and other saints who had been flung to lions rather than violate God's commands to please Kings, he ingenuously remarked that these holy men, being endowed with the gift of prophecy, were enabled to foretell beforehand that God would not allow the lions to do them any harm.

"We, however," he added, "have no assurance, if the Sultan should put us in the fort, for applying the Divine Law without fear of man, that Allah would send an angel to release us." It is probable that the Sultans themselves, in signing and enforcing all these Edicts against the Moslem laws of slavery, in order to conciliate mighty infidel powers, have found, and will continue to find, much comfort in this pleasant and useful doctrine of "takiah."

The grounds on which slaves are now freed by the Sultan and myself are twofold: (1) illegal purchase or importation, and (2) cruelty. It frequently happens that slaves come here with complaints of one kind or another (many are sent by the English missionaries, to whom they go even in greater numbers than to Her Majesty's Agency, and who always send them on to myself), and that it transpires on inquiry that they have either been imported since the Decree of Seyyid Khalifa, or changed masters by sale, gift, or bequest, since the Decree of Seyyid Ali — both of which, owing to real or pretended ignorance, are, I regret to say, constantly disobeyed. Complaints of cruelty are a good deal more frequent; but many of the cases brought before me are purely frivolous, and often amount merely to a blow or to a mild castigation with the stick for impertinence, laziness, assaults on other slaves, or some equally trifling matter. Once, for instance, a concubine complained to me that her master had brought home a second slave girl, and wanted either to be emancipated herself, or to be given, if her rival were not instantly dismissed, a separate house to live in with her children. On her master's agreeing to this she objected, because the house was in the country and was not in town, and she ultimately carried her point, and drove the rival concubine from the field. When, however, any case of real cruelty comes to my notice, and the slave shows either marks of severe beating, or of having been insufficiently fed, or been made to work when physically unfit, or complains of the withholding of any of the customary indulgences, I either free him myself if he belongs to the mainland, or send him, if a native of Zanzibar, to the Sultan, with a request that he may be freed, and his master punished according to the merits of the case; and His Highness has hitherto in every instance most readily carried out my wishes. I should add that the same procedure is followed in the case of slaves sold or imported contrary to the Sultan's Decree; and, further, that since 1890, under the agreement between Seyyid Khalifa and Sir Gerald Portal of the 13th September, 1889, all persons, whatever their origin, born in Pemba and Zanzibar, are born free. I have not so far insisted on this last measure, for it, at present, only affects very young children; and there is always the obvious danger that some owners (I trust not very many) might reply that, if these children are not their slaves, they are under no obligation to maintain or assist their slave mothers in maintaining them. Such a contention would, of course, be most inhuman, and quite opposed to the Mahommedan religion; but it might not be easy for the Sultan or myself to appeal to the Mahommedan law in this respect, after having ourselves disregarded it in so many others. The question as to how these children's rights shall be asserted, and what compensation, if any, shall be assigned to their present masters for providing for them till they grow up, will, however, become more pressing every year. My own inclination would be, whilst treating them in every other respect (civil rights, &c.) as absolute freemen, to apprentice them for a term of years — seven, ten, or any other reasonable period — after the age of (say) 15, to their parents' master, and thus make them pay back in useful labour the cost of their maintenance during childhood.

The following European views on the reaction of the African slave to the condition of slavery and attainment of freedom seem particularly harsh, and, no doubt, in the context of the later twentieth century, would be termed 'racist'. First, from Sir Arthur Hardinge to Lord Salisbury.

A slave in a moment of pique, or yielding to the sudden impulses to which the African like a child, is very prone, will frequently run away from his old surroundings and afterwards repent at leisure — and thus suddenly severing his old ties with his old home toils along on the Uganda road with a weight of 60 lbs on his head, under the strict discipline of a European caravan leader, impatient of malingering or idleness, will doubt perhaps whether he was not better off in his own holding on the Zanzibar plantation and, amidst the dreary steppes of Masailand, sigh regretfully, as does every true Swahili, for the scent of the cocoa-nuts and the spice trees.

FOCP 7077/103, 23 April 1898

Then an extract from F. D. Lugard's *The Rise of Our East African Empire*, London, 1893, Vol. I, pp. 309-10.

These savages do not think or act as we do. They are, in truth, like 'dumb driven cattle'. With the slave caravan they suffer uncomplainingly starvation, the scourge and all the painted horrors of so many writers. They meet a European safari, and they hide in the jungle and rejoin the Slavers. Like cattle, they will face any misery, but dread the unknown. They are brought on by us, — fed, clothed, and spoken kindly to; they bolt. Why? Perhaps they are suspicious of what all this means, and as in the dumb brute's instinct to wander which makes them go. They wander off as cattle do, regardless of state and food, of danger from lions, or danger of a cruel master, instead of a kind one. The very immediate present is the only thought, and sooner than march tomorrow to the unknown, they slip off today, and follow the caged bird's instinct, and, like it, they perish in their ill-advised liberty; but who blames the foolish bird?

And lastly a report from Mr. J. P. Farler, Commissioner for Pemba,

Since the restraints imposed by their Arab masters have been removed, Pemba has become one huge brothel, the women being worse than the men. They seem to have but half-human souls, and with the subtlety of savages, the passions and physical strength of adults, they have only the intelligence of the child to restrain them.

FOCP 7823/47, 19 April 1901

IV
NORTHEASTERN AFRICA AND THE HORN

The ramifications of the slave trade in the vast area of northeastern Africa and the Horn are not easy to delineate, but that the scale of the trade was immense is not in doubt, nor the difficulty in suppressing it.

One of the earliest references by a European to the slave trade in the Red Sea area is in *A Voyage in the Indian Ocean and to Bengal and A Voyage in the Red Sea in 1790* (translated from the French), Boston, 1803, p. 221, by L. de Grandpré, who visited there in 1790. Speaking of his visit to Mocha, in Arabia, he states that the Arabs supplied their seraglios with females from Abyssinia, 'of whom whole cargoes arrive at a time'.

I have seen among them some women of exquisite beauty; they are black, but nothing is so bewitching as their form, or so elegant and graceful as their motions. I was one day so struck with one of these slaves as she landed from her dhow, that I instantly made a proposal of my Bannian to purchase her: she lifted up a dirty piece of coarse blue cloth, which served her for a veil, and exposed a most charming figure. I inquired her price, but the merchant, seeing it was a Christian who wanted her, answered that he supposed my Bannian to have spoken for some Musulman, and refused to treat with me.

Sir Richard F. Burton, in disguise, penetrated the holy city of Mecca and was able to view the slave market. This description is from his *Pilgrimage to Al-Madinah and Meccah*, London, 1893, p. 252.

It is a large street roofed with matting, and full of coffee-houses. The merchandise sat in rows, parallel with the walls. The prettiest girls occupied the highest benches, below were the plainer sort, and lowest of all the boys. They were all gaily dressed in pink and other light-coloured muslins, with transparent veils over their heads; and, whether from the effect of such unusual splendour, or from the re-action succeeding to their terrible land-journey and sea-voyage, they appeared perfectly happy, laughing loudly, talking unknown tongues, and quizzing purchasers, even during the delicate operation of purchasing. There were some pretty Gallas, douce-looking Abyssinians, and Africans of various degrees of hideousness, from the half-Arab Somal to the baboon-like Sawahili. The highest price of which I could hear was £60. And here I matured a resolve to strike, if favoured by fortune, a death-blow at a trade which is eating into the vitals of industry in Eastern Africa. The reflection was pleasant, — the idea that the humble Haji, contemplating the scene from his donkey, might become the instrument of the total abolition of this pernicious traffic. What would have become of that pilgrim had the crowd in the slave-market guessed his intentions?

And according to Consul Stanley in Jeddah, to Consul-General Colquhoun,

In Jeddah slaves are publicly sold by auction every morning, when they are stripped almost naked, and examined by anyone wishing to purchase. The fact that a great number of these cannot speak a work of Arabic proves that fresh ones are constantly imported.

SP Vol. LXXI, 1863, No. 309, 21 January 1862.

The following account of the slave trade in Kordofan in the Soudan, at the mid-nineteenth century, is from Captain W. Peel's *A Ride Through the Nubian Desert*, London, 1852, pp. 79–81.

"The trade of Kordofan is chiefly in gum arabic, which exudes from the sond trees, and is collected at certain seasons of the year. Slaves, also, are bought and captured in the neighbourhood. I will copy an extract from my note-book on these unhappy creatures: — 'Monday morning, November 10, 1851 — Scene opposite my windows, which look into the Government court-yard. Five male slaves just arrived, their necks in a wooden triangle, at the end of a long heavy pole, which on the march was of course attached to a camel — one female slave, bound by the feet. I believe the number of slaves brought every year to Khartoum and Labeyed, and thence sent into Egypt, is very great. Some are also sent from Darfoor to Siout. I have just ascertained that these few were caught by the Arabs, in some mountains to the southward. In the afternoon, these slaves were stripped, examined, made to walk — in fact, critically examined like beasts — in the same Government court-yard. And how did they behave — like beasts? I watched them closely, unseen, and cannot conceive how men could have behaved with more propriety, or shown more touching dignity. There was no fear, nor was there any momentary pride of the man, to show his muscular figure: they held themselves mechanically, let others bend their limbs, and marched no further than the very line. When finished, they wrapped their scanty clothing with decency round their waists, and took no notice of the flowing robe, the gorgeous turban of their masters. As men, physically, they were their superior; in heart and feeling, it is mockery to make comparison; in courage, unquestionably not inferior; but they have no self-reliance or moral strength, and in the onward march of·the world, from the position of their country and its climate, have been left behind.

"Kordofan, on its conquest by the Egyptians, some thirty years ago, was a rich and populous negro country; it is now quite the reverse. The excesses of the troops and exactions of the Government have ruined it.

Mr Bayard Taylor, writing to the *New York Tribune* from Khartoum in 1852 — this appeared in the *Anti-Slavery Reporter*, 2 August 1852 — reported as regards slavery in the Soudan, that

The traffic in slaves has decreased very much of late. The wealthy Egyptians still purchase slaves, and will continue to do so, till the "institution" is wholly abolished, but the despotic rule exercised by the Pasha in Nubia has had the effect of greatly lessening the demand. Vast numbers of Nubians go into Egypt, where they are engaged as domestic servants, and their paid labour, cheap as it is, is found more profitable than the unpaid service of negro slaves. Besides, the tax on the latter has been greatly increased, so that merchants find the commodity less profitable than gum or ivory. Ten years ago, the duty paid at Assouan was 30 piastres for a negro, and 50 for an Abyssinian: at present, it is 350 the former, and 550 for the latter, while the tax can be wholly avoided by making the slave free. Prices have risen in consequence, and the traffic is proportionately diminished. The Government, probably, derives as large a revenue as ever from it, on account of the increased tax, so that it has seemed to satisfy the demands of some of the European powers by restricting the trade, while it actually loses nothing thereby. The Government slave-hunts in the interior, however, are no longer carried on. The greater part of the slaves brought here are purchased from the Galla and Shongollo tribes on the borders of Abyssinia, or from the Shillooks and Dinkas on the White Nile. The captives taken in the wars between the various tribes are invariably sold. The Abyssinian girls, who are in great demand among the Egyptians for wives, are frequently sold by their own parents. They are treated with great respect, and their lot is, probably, no worse than that of any Arab or Turkish female. The more beautiful of them often bring from 200 to 500 dollars. In fact, among the Mohammedans in general, marriage is always a matter of bargain and sale. Ordinary household servants may be had at from one to two thousand piastres. My dragoman, Achmet, purchased a small girl, the other day, for 1,200 piastres, to be brought up in his household. He intends making her free, as he says this is a good thing, according to his religion; but the true reason, I suspect, is the tax at Assouan.

The Egyptians rarely maltreat their slaves, and instances of cruelty are much less frequent among them than among the Europeans settled here. The latter became so notorious for their violence, that the Government was obliged to establish a law, forbidding any Frank to strike his slave; but, in case of disobedience, to send him before the cadi, or judge, who would decide on the proper punishment. With few exceptions, the Europeans here are even worse than the natives. They have their *harems*, and practise every species of dissipation and debauchery. The German priests here, under their most worthy vicar, Dr. Knoblecher, are true representatives of the European character and the European name, and their influence will, in time, heal the baneful moral leprosy which has fallen on others.

The Egyptian merchants, who are located here as agents for houses in Cairo, consider themselves as worse than exiles, and indemnify themselves by sensual indulgence for being obliged to remain in a country which they detest. They live in large houses, keep their harems of inky slaves, eat, drink, and smoke away their languid and wearisome days. All they need for such a life is so cheap, that their love of gain does not suffer thereby. One of the richest merchants in the place gave me an account of his housekeeping. He has a large mud palace, a garden, and twenty servants and slaves, to maintain which, he spends 8,000 piastres ($400) yearly. He pays his servants twenty piastres a month, and his slaves also; at least, so he told me, but I do not believe it. I have never yet seen the Arab who would give money away when he could help it.

The following account is taken from *The Heart of Africa*, New York, 1874, Vol. II, pp. 418-31 by Dr George Schweinfurth who travelled in the southern Soudan in the early 1870s. The *Seribas* were the village encampments and their enclosures into which the slave-raiders collected their slaves.

As regards the price paid for slaves, I can only report what I personally witnessed in the Seribas. Copper and calico are used as the principal mediums of exchange. Calico is very fluctuating in its value, which is always first reduced to its equivalent in copper. In 1871 thirty rottoli of copper in Dehm Nduggo and twenty-five rottoli in the Bongo and Dyoor districts was taken for young slaves of both sexes of the class called "sittahsi" (literally, six spans high), meaning children of eight or ten years of age; thus making the average price in this country, according to the value of copper in Khartoom, to be about 7½ Maria Theresa dollars (1*l.* 10s.); particularly pretty women-slaves called "nadeef," *i. e.* clean or pure, fetch nearly double that price, and are very rarely procured for exportation, because they are in great demand amongst the numerous settlers in the country. Strong adult women, who are ugly, are rather cheaper than the young girls, whilst old women are worth next to nothing, and can be bought for a mere bagatelle. Full-grown men are rarely purchased as slaves, being troublesome to control and difficult of transport. Slaves in the East are usually in demand as *objets de luxe,* and consequently lead an idle life, and are not valued according to their capablities for labour.

In consequence of the glut of wares in the market during the winter of 1871, the quoted value of slaves rose to almost double that of the previous year, and very high prices were paid in cotton stuffs. As much as four or six pieces of the ordinary sort (damoor) were paid for the "sittahsi," each piece measuring twenty-four yards in length, and worth two Maria Theresa dollars in Khartoom. Next to white cotton materials firearms are a very favourite means of payment, and bring in a far larger proportional profit. For an ordinary double-barrelled gun of French or Belgian manufacture, a slave-dealer can purchase two or three sittahsi, and if the weapon has gilt facings he can sometimes obtain as many as five for it.

The price of slaves in Khartoom at that time might be reckoned to be at least six times their original cost; of course it will be understood that the value would be regulated to a great extent by the more or less severe measures taken by the local government for the suppression of the trade; but at the time of my departure from Khartoom, at a period when the market was tolerably unrestrained, no slave could be obtained for less than forty Maria Theresa dollars, and that was the lowest price given for elderly women only fit for household service.

The slaves brought from the Bahr-el-Ghazal districts vary in value according to their nationality. The Bongo are the most prized, as they are easily taught and are docile and faithful, and are, besides, good-looking and industrious. True Niam-niam, especially young girls, are, however, much dearer than the best Bongo slaves, but they are so extremely rare as hardly to admit of having a price quoted. The Mittoo are of little value, being ugly, lean, and incapable of enduring fatigue or even of undertaking any regular work. No amount of good living or kind treatment can overcome the love of freedom of the Babuckur; they take every oportunity of effecting an escape, and can only be secured by fetters and by the yoke;* the same may also be said of the Loobah and Abaka. The demand for slaves in the Seribas through which I travelled would alone suffice to support a very flourishing trade. Numerically the Mohammedan settlers bear a high ratio to the native population, and in some of the western territories,

as amongst the Kredy, Golo and Sehre, they are actually considerably
in excess of the total number of natives, who only consist of bearers
and agricultural labourers. Taken one with another every Nubian
possesses about three slaves, and thus it may easily be conceived that
the computation is not too high that places the total number of
private slaves in the country at between 50,000 and 60,000. These
private slaves are quite distinct from those that are kept in store and
used as merchandise; they may be divided into four categories: —

1. Boys from seven to ten years of age, who are employed to carry
guns and ammunition: every Nubian soldier possesses at least one of
these juvenille armour-bearers. When they get older they are
included in my next category.

2. The second class includes the greater part of the full-grown
natives in the Seribas. They are termed "Farookh," "Narakeek," or
"Bazingir," and, being provided with guns, form a kind of Nizzam,
whose duty it is to accompany the natives in all their expeditions,
whether for war or for trading purposes. These black soldiers
constitute nearly half the fighting force in all the Seribas, and play a
prominent part in time of war. It is the duty of the Farookh to scour
the negro villages in search of corn, to assemble the bearers, and to
keep under coercion any that are refractory in the wilderness. In
every action the hardest work is put upon their shoulders, and they
have not only to sustain the chief brunt of any actual conflict with the
savages, but to provide for the safe custody of all prisoners. If the
controllers of the Seribas had a sufficient number of these Farookh,
they might well dispense altogether with their Nubian soldiers, except
for one reason, to which I have already referred, viz. the constant
danger of their running away, a risk that makes them practically less
reliable than the Nubians, who never think of such a thing, and even
if they did, would only join another company. The Farookh have
wives, children, and land in the Seribas, and some of the elder
amongst them have even slave boys of their own to carry their guns.
Their ranks are largely increased after every Niam-niam expedition,
as numbers of young natives will often voluntarily attach themselves
to the Nubians, and, highly delighted at getting a cotton shirt and
gun of their own, will gladly surrender themselves to slavery,
attracted moreover by the hope of finding better food in the Seribas
than their own native wildernesses can produce. The mere offer of
these simple inducements in any part of the Niam-niam lands would
be sufficient to gather a whole host of followers and vassals, and
during our journey I myself received proposals to join our band from
young people in all parts of the country. I mention this circumstance
just to illustrate my opinion of how easily the Egyptian Government

might, without using any compulsion, enlist here as many soldiers as it required. I am persuaded that, without any difficulty, whole regiments of Nizzam troops might be raised from amongst the Niam-niam in the course of comparatively a very few days.

3. The third class of private slaves is formed of the women who are kept in the houses. Every soldier has one of these slaves, and sometimes more, in which case one is advanced to the position of favourite, whilst the rest are employed in the ordinary routine of preparing meal, or in the tedious process of baking kissere. These women are passed like dollars from hand to hand, a proceeding which is a prolific source of the rapid spread of those loathsome disorders by which the lands within the jurisdiction of the Seribas have been infested ever since their subjugation by the Khartoomers. In accordance with the universal rule in the Mohammedan Soudan, the children of a slave are reared as legitimate, and the mother receives the title of wife. The daily conversation of the Nubian mercenaries is a continual proof that their thoughts are always running on their slaves both male and female. If a quarrel arises amongst a group of people, one is certain to be correct in surmising that some slave or other is being reclaimed or the payment due for her is being demanded; or if there is a sudden uproar, the burden of the cry is sure to be, "A slave has run away!" "Kummarah olloroh," shout the Bongo, and "Ollomollo, ollomollo," resounds from every side. Many and many a time have I been roused from my slumbers in the early morning by such cries as these, and it is one of the occupations of the Seriba people and their negroes to hunt down and recapture these runaway women. Hunger often obliges the fugitives to take refuge in a strange Seriba; here they are looked upon as lucky windfalls, and are either seized by force or are quietly disposed of to the itinerant Gellahbas; and if the rightful owner subsequently appears to claim his property, a violent squabble will inevitably be the result. These slaves are thus the subject of one incessant wrangling; and if a slave absent herself only temporarily without the consent of her master, she will at once excite his jealousy, displeasure, and mistrust.

The single slave of the poorer soldiers is a regular drudge, or maid-of-all work: she has to bring water from the well in great pitchers, which she carries on her head; she does all the washing, if there is anything to wash; she grinds the corn upon the murhaga, makes the dough, roasts the kissere on the doka, and finally prepares the melah, a horrible greasy concoction of water, sesame-oil or pounded sesame, bamia-pods, and corchorus leaves, beautifully seasoned with cayenne pepper and alkali. Not only has she to do the sweeping of the whole house, but she has to get wood from the wilderness, and, when on a journey, to supply the want of any other bearer by carrying all the lumber of her lord and master. In the larger households, however, of the more important people, such as controllers or agents, where slaves are numerous, each woman has her own allotted task, and a large number of boys is employed, who follow their master on his travels, each carrying a single weapon, either a gun, a pistol, or a sword. From all this some little idea may be gained of the unwieldy crowd that must necessarily be attached to every march undertaken by the Nubian mercenaries. To a force of 200 soldiers on our Niam-niam expedition there were as many as 300 women and boys; a party which, as well as immoderately increasing the length of the procession, by the clatter of their cooking utensils and their everlasting wrangling (scenes of which I have already given some il- lustration), kept up a perpetual turmoil which at times threatened a hopeless confusion.

The rude and primitive manner of grinding corn employed throughout the Mohammedan Soudan contributes more than may at first sight seem credible to perpetuate the immense demand for female slave labour. The very laborious process is performed by pounding the grain on a large stone, called murhaga, by means of a smaller stone held in the hand; it is the only method of grinding corn known to the majority of African nations, and is so slow that by the hardest day's work a woman is able to prepare only a sufficient quantity of meal for five or six men. A mill worked by oxen has been erected by the Government in Khartoom, not only for the use of the troops, but also to enable private individuals to have their corn ground at a moderate price; but in spite of this provision the durra- corn is still pounded on the murhaga in all the houses; not a single resident takes advantage of the improved facility that is offered. Until this lavish waste of human strength is suppressed, either by the introduction of mechanical handmills or by putting a tax upon the murhaga, no hope is to be entertained of any diminution in the demand for female slaves. This is but one instance, yet it may suffice to show how gradually and consistently one must set to work ultimately to gain the suppression of slavery in the Soudan: nowhere can old institutions be declared to be abolished, until new institutions have been provided to take their place.

4. In my fourth and last category I would include all slaves of both sexes who are employed exclusively in husbandry. Only the men in more important situations, such as the controllers of the Seribas, the clerks, the dragomen (generally natives who have been brought up like Arabs in Khartoom), the Fakis, and the colonised Gellahbas

actually cultivate the soil and possess cattle; the poorer people being content with a little occasional gardening and the possession of a few goats and fowls. Old women, who are too weak for anything else, are employed to weed the fields, and at harvest time the Farookh are called to their assistance. Statute labour as applied to agriculture is nowhere demanded of the natives, although it would really act less disadvantageously on the condition of the population than the arbitrary system that allows any controller of a Seriba to seize the children from the native villages and dispose of them to the Gellahbas, a proceeding that is generally carried out as a punishment for offences like dishonesty, treachery, or attempts to abscond.

The remote position of the Seribas places the controllers far beyond any authority, and makes them quite independent of the jurisdiction of the chiefs of the trading-firms, who are most of them settled in Khartoom without much care for either their own advantage or for that of the country; it thus becomes necessary to appoint trustworthy people to the post, and consequently the head-controllers are in many cases slaves who have been reared in their master's house. A controller has every opportunity if he pleases of coming to an arrangement with the soldiers and other officials, and in concert with them of acting very much to his chief's disadvantage; or he might sell the negroes on his territories to the Gellahbas, turn the proceeds into copper, and retire as a rich man to Darfoor, already a place of refuge for many delinquents from the Egyptian Soudan.

The sub-controllers and agents in the subsidiary Seribas are, on the other hand, far less trustworthy; their position is often held only for a temporary period, and consequently their interests are not so firmly bound up with those of their chiefs as those of his former slaves. Then, too, the smaller Seribas are often so far apart that the Vokeel can transact all their business without any supervision from the head controller; all this is well known to the itinerant slave-dealers, who have a special preference for visiting these minor settlements, because they are aware that they can there buy up numbers of boys and girls, disregardful of the fact that, as future bearers and agricultural labourers, the children are vassals belonging to the soil, and form part and parcel of the property of the head of the firm.

After thus considering slave-labour in its separate branches, and gaining some idea of the immense and wasteful expenditure of human energy that goes on in the Seribas of the Khartoomers, we may turn our attention to the numerical proportion of the foreign settlers (with whom must be included their private slaves) to the actual aboriginal population. The following table is founded upon a careful calculation; the results are given in round numbers, as fuller details would demand more space than could be afforded here.

Proportions of the POPULATION *in the District of the* KHARTOOMERS'
SERIBAS *on the Bahr-el-Ghazal.*

CONSUMERS.

Nubian soldiers, recruited in Khartoom and consisting of natives of Dongola, Sheygieh, Sennaar, Kordofan, various Bedouins, &c .	5,000
Black slave troops (Farookh)*	5,000
Fellow-boarders with the Nubian idlers from the Soudan, living here in order to procure corn cheaply and without any trouble . .	1,000
Gellahbas settled in Dar Ferteet, and agents in the Seribas, Fakis, &c.	2,000
Itinerant Gellahbas, who enter the country in the winter . .	2,000
Private slaves belonging to the colonised Mohammedan population	40,000
TOTAL . .	55,000

PRODUCERS.

Bongo	100,000
Mittoo (including Loobah, Madi, &c.)	30,000
Dyoor	10,000
Golo	6,000
Sehre	4,000
Kredy	20,000
Small tribes of natives belonging to the immediate environs of the Seribas, such as the Dembo, Bimberry, Manga, &c.	20,000
TOTAL . .	190,000

In the next place let us turn our attention to those slaves who are
regarded as actual merchandise, and who are dragged into bondage
from the Upper Nile lands solely for purposes of profit. In order to
demonstrate how important at the present time is the part taken by
the district of the Gazelle in the entire African slave-trade, I will take
a brief survey of the sources which all the year round supply the
endless succession of the dealers with fresh stores of living wares, and
which, branching off into three great highways to the north, yield up
their very life-blood to gratify the insatiable and luxurious demands
of Egypt, Arabia, Persia, and Asiatic Turkey. Previous travellers
have estimated the total of the annual traffic in this immense region
to be 25,000, but I shall show by a very summary reckoning that this

* I should point out that the total number of soldiers maintained in the
Bahr-el-Ghazal district by the twelve great mercantile firms in Khartoom
amounts to 11,000. I have here given the lowest computation.

is far too low a computation. The three currents for the slave-trade in north-east Africa (a region corresponding to what may be geographically termed the "Nile district") are the natural highways of the Nile and the Red Sea, and the much frequented caravan roads that, traversing the deserts at no great distance to the west of the Nile, find their outlet either in Siout or near Cairo. As a proof of how little these roads even now are known, I may mention that when in the summer of 1871, a caravan with 2000 slaves arrived direct from Wadai, it caused quite a sensation in the neighbourhood of the pyramids of Gizeh; it was supposed to have traversed a geographical *terra incognita*, and it divided and dispersed itself as mysteriously as it came. It is far more difficult to place the deserts under inspection than the ocean, and this is especially the case in the vicinity of a river, where a caravan can easily supply itself with water for many days. The borders of a desert are like the coasts of an unnavigable ocean. The plan, however, of establishing a system of control along the borders of the Nile Valley, corresponding to the coastguard cruisers on our seas, has never yet been tried.

The following are the territories that form the sources of the slave-trade in North-Eastern Africa (Nile district): —

1. The Galla countries to the south of Abyssinia, between latitude 3° and 8°N. The outlets from them are: *(a) viâ* Shoa to Zeyla; *(b) viâ* Godyam through Abyssinia to Matamma and Suakin, or to Massowa and smaller unguarded coast towns; *(c) viâ* Fazogl to Sennaar, where the largest market is not in, but above Khartoom, in a place called Mussalemia; the merchandise brought by this route is abundant and valuable. According to the reports of the Abyssinian collectors of customs the number of slaves in Matamma (Gallabat) amounted in 1865 alone to 18,000.

2. The second source is found amongst the Berta negroes above Fazogl, and amongst the Dinka above Sennaar, between the White and Blue Niles. These are likewise carried to Mussalemia and Khartoom, but in no considerable numbers.

3. The Agow, in the heart of Abyssinia between Tigre and Amhara, together with the people on the north-west frontier of the Abyssinian highland, are also exposed to plunder of the persons of their sons, on account of their disorganised condition and their position on the wild border-land. The channel for their dispersion is across the Red Sea to Djidda.

4. The upper district of the White Nile, inclusive of the Albert and Victoria Lakes, though the slave-trade really begins at latitude 5°N. The expedition of Sir Samuel Baker has stopped this source. The annual produce in the most favourable years did not exceed 1000.

5. The supply of slaves in the upper district of the Bahr-el-Ghazal is chiefly derived from the Bongo, Mittoo, and Babuckur. For the last twelve years the Gazelle has never been navigated by more than twenty boats. On their return journeys the soldiers of the ivory merchants carry their own slaves with them as payment and perquisites; but it is very rare for a boat to carry more than twenty or thirty of these slaves, so that the annual transport of slaves to Khartoom by this route never exceeded from 400 to 600. This fact is perfectly authentic, and thus it may be seen that even before Sir Samuel Baker's expedition put a stop to it altogether, the slave trade that was carried on down the river was quite insignificant compared to the overland traffic. For years there has been a public prohibition against bringing slaves down the White Nile into Khartoom, and ever and again stronger repressive measures have been introduced, which, however, have only had the effect of raising the land traffic to a premium; but as a general rule the Egyptian officials connive at the use of this comparatively unimportant channel of the trade, and pocket a quiet little revenue for themselves by demanding a sum varying from two to five dollars a head as hush-money. This expense, together with the continual risk of the property being confiscated in Khartoom, has always prevented the river trade from reaching a very flourishing condition; at all events, the Egyptian Government has hitherto had the best of it. Consuls from England, France, Germany, and Austria have been, and are still in residence at Khartoom, and a Copt was also temporarily appointed as consular agent for America; it was therefore an easy matter for the Egyptian officials to feign in the eyes of the world at large a wonderful amount of zeal and energy in the suppression of the slave-trade, especially as every confiscation threw the whole cargo into their hands; for the slaves were never sent back into their native lands, but the full-grown men were turned into soldiers, whilst the young girls and boys were divided at discretion amongst the troops of the garrison. In these transactions a formidable bond was always entered into by the receiver, from whom the former owner was at liberty at any time to re-purchase the slave.

6. As we have already seen, the great source of the slave-trade is to be found in the negro-countries to the south of Darfoor, which are included under the name of Dar Ferteet. The natives, who for the last forty years have been exposed to the rapacity of the slave-dealers, and have been annually exported to the number of from 12,000 to 15,000 souls, belong to the Kredy tribes; but the great bulk of the slaves come from the western Niam-niam territories, where the powerful King Mofio (whose residence is about under latitude 7°N. and longitude 24°E.) carries off on his own account, from the neighbouring nations

who are not Niam-niam, large numbers of slaves, and sells them to the Gellahbas, by whom they are conveyed by the overland routes already mentioned across Kordofan to Aboo Harras in the Egyptian dominons. There are other routes that lead direct to Darfoor, whence caravans start twice a year to Siout. Kordofan is in many ways in direct communication with the most important markets of the slave trade; the following being the most frequented caravan roads: *(a)* from Aboo Harras to Khartoom *viâ* El-Obeïd; *(b)* from Aboo Harras eastwards to Mussalemia through Sennaar; *(c)* from Aboo Harras across the Begudah steppes to Dongola *viâ* El-Safy; *(d)* from Aboo Harras to Berber along the Nile, for the purpose either of crossing the great Nubian Desert or of keeping farther to the east across the Red Sea. All these routes are associated to me by the many reminiscences of slave-transport which I recall as having myself witnessed there.

7. A final and by no means unimportant source of the slave-trade is found in the mountain lands south of Kordofan. The general term for the negroes of these parts is Nooba,* a people that are much in demand on account of their beauty and intelligence. It was in these Nooba mountains that, after his bloody conquest of Kordofan, Mehemet Ali, the great reformer and usurper in Egypt, allowed kidnapping to be a legitimate source for the State revenue. From the slaves thus obtained he formed black regiments, by means of which he was to subdue the insalubrious Soudan, and paid his officers and subordinates with a portion of the plunder.†

As the Egyptian Government itself was the first to teach its subjects to kidnap slaves, it behoves it now in these more humane times to make amends for all its past delinquencies, and I most cordially acknowledge that the present ruler, with all the resources at his command, is striving most honourably to accomplish the task.

The following sketch drawn up by Colonel Gordon for The Anti-Slavery Society in early 1880, and printed by the Society in May of that year in London, outlines the story of the suppression of the slave trade in the Sudan, and of Gordon's role in it while Governor-General of the Sudan and Red Sea Provinces, 1877–80.

"You are, no doubt, aware that in the year 1856 or 1857 several Europeans pushed up towards the Equator from Kartoum, and

---

* This word must not be confounded with Nubian, a word which has come down from antiquity, and which, like the term Egypt, did not originally apply to the inhabitants of the Nile Valley.

† If this account of slave capture in the time of Mehemet Ali should appear incredible, I would refer the reader to a book that contains the narrative of an eye-witness: Pallame, 'Travels in Kordofan', London, 1844.

established stations in the Bahr Gazelle district, for the purchase of ivory from the negro tribes, and that these Europeans had under them escorts of Soudan population to protect these establishments. Over these establishments the Europeans placed natives as their agents. As these establishments grew in size the European supervision over them grew less severe, and the native agents began to see that getting slaves was more profitable for them than getting ivory for their European masters. Having arms and ammunition through the interest of the Europeans, these natives soon opened such a trade in slaves that the scandal became too great, and the Europeans left the concern, and handed over, for payment, their rights to their vakeels or agents. These vakeels or agents entered into engagements with the Soudan Government to pay so much a year as rent for these establishments, and were further allowed to buy arms and ammunition from the Soudan arsenals. Then arose the state of things which is most graphically described in Baker's 'Albert Nyanza.'

"The Soudan Government began to see that their power over these establishments was lessening day by day, and they determined to try and bring them under subjection; accordingly, when Sir S. Baker went up in 1869 to govern the districts south of 5°N. latitude, Ismail Pacha, the ex-Khedive, sent up an expedition to the head-quarters of these establishments in Bahr Gazelle. The most powerful of the agents of these establishments was a man who had been employed by the Europeans, and was known by the name of Sebehr Rahama. Of course, neither he nor his colleagues wished to have any Government interference with them. Accordingly Sebehr, seeking some pretext, fell out with the commander of the Khedive's troops, and, attacking him, killed him and all the troops. — *Vide* Schweinfurth's 'Heart of Africa.' Appendix, 'Sebehr.'

"Sebehr was thus in open hostility to the Government, and the Government could not see how they could get at him at Bahr Gazelle without a great campaign. Sebehr, on his part, wrote all excuses for his action, and the matter slept; but the ex-Khedive saw that things were getting serious, for Sebehr, seeing his power, began to move down towards Darfour. The Khedive, seeing that unless he co-operated in the annexation of Darfour, Sebehr would conquer it on his own account, determined to aid in this annexation, and accordingly Sebehr and his troops and the Khedival troops conquered Darfour. Sebehr, falling out with the commander of the Khedive's troops, and thinking he was all powerful with his money, appealed to the Khedive, and applied for leave to come to Cairo. This was granted him, and Sebehr left, having agreed with his people to revolt against the Government on receiving his orders to that effect.

"The slave dealers remained quiet in Bahr Gazelle, waiting orders from Sebehr. Of course Sebehr was retained at Cairo, but he was still a power, for, with the sole exception of the Ex-Khedive, he had the Pachas with him, as well as the people of the land.

"A revolt in Darfour in 1877 brought me in contact with these people of Sebehr, and I managed to detach some of the chiefs from the others.

"I sent up troops to Bahr Gazelle, and nominally the slave dealers accepted the Government Rule. However, in May, 1878, Sebehr (seeing he was not likely to return, unless something was done), wrote and ordered the revolt.

"The slave dealers rose under Sebehr's son 'Souleyman,' and killed the Khedival troops, and captured all the ammunition and two cannon, and declared their independence, until Sebehr was given back to them. I sent up Gessi Pacha, in August, 1878, but till January, 1879, he was delayed through the high floods; he came near the slave dealers' hold on 1st January, 1879. The slave dealers, who had 8,000 or 9,000 troops, attacked Gessi and his 3,000 men with fury. Both Gessi and Souleyman had two guns each, and Gessi had intrenched himself. The slave dealers left 600 dead around the stockade, and after their defeat they fell back some 1,200 yards and made a fort. Gessi and they remained face to face for two months, when Gessi got fresh ammunition, and captured the wells which supplied the slave dealers with water, who then fell back. (During this two months the slave dealers attacked Gessi over and over again, but were always defeated.)

"Gessi then started in pursuit, and after a sharp action captured the second position of the slave dealers, and found the letters of Sebehr Rahama, which had ordered the slave dealers to rise. Gessi then pursued them, and every one of the ringleaders was shot. Immense droves of slaves were released, and the whole vast system of the slave trade utterly destroyed.

"The finale took place in July, 1879.

"The slave dealers were killed by hundreds by the exasperated natives, who retaliated for the cruel hunting to which they had been subjected.

"The last telegram, sent me 24th June, 1879, from the Ex-Khedive Ismail Pacha was congratulations about this affair, and the promotion of Gessi to be Pacha. During the time I governed the Soudan, Ismail Pacha supported me through thick and thin against his own Pachas, and against his own people. Piles of petitions came to H.H. against me; he would not listen to them.

"The new Khedive has never mentioned Sebehr's name or the

slave-trade revolt, has never thanked me, or any one concerned. Sebehr was tried by several Pachas on the captured letters proving his complicity with the revolt, the documents were sent to Cairo, but no action was taken, and Sebehr now gets £100 a month!

"Mr. A. B. Wylde has stated that from 20,000 to 50,000 slaves passed the Red Sea every year, and I have no hesitation in saying that 20,000 slaves have for twelve years past come down from Bahr Gazelle and Darfour, and that two-thirds of the Darfour population have been taken into slavery!

"No one can conceive the quantity of skulls which mark the slave routes. It is simply appalling.

"It is no use talking about the past, what is to be done for the future?

"Raouf Pacha (vide 'Ismalia' by Baker, Appendix 'Raouf Bey') has been appointed to the Soudan. Baker will tell you what he knows of him. I turned him out of Harar for oppression, and he is the Pacha who treacherously strangled the old Ameer of Harar who surrendered to him.

"Is it likely he will discourage the slave trade? Will he not, in all probability, encourage its renewal?

"What is to be done?"

The question of what is to be done is contained in a further letter to the Anti-Slavery Society written by Colonel Gordon on the eve of his departure for India, under date 30 April 1880.

"I have learned with equal pain and indignation that the Khedive and his subordinate officers have permitted the resuscitation of the slave trade in Darfour and the other provinces of central and equatorial Africa, and that fresh parties of slave-hunters are forming at Obeid in Kordofan, and that every order which I gave concerning the suppression of this abomination has been cancelled.

"The two missionaries — Wilson and Felkin — who have lately come down from Uganda, passed through these districts, and they tell me that the slave-hunters are all ready to start once more upon their detestable trade, and that there is a very strong feeling abroad that all the Europeans, including of course Gessi and the other officers who acted under me, are about to be turned out of the country. This report, even if it be untrue, will largely serve to lower the authority of the European officers, and to render their work more difficult.

"This news is very disheartening, especially when one realises the immense misery which will ensue to the remnants of these poor tribes of helpless negroes.

"I verily believe that nearly two-thirds of the population have already been dragged off into slavery, and I have myself stopped caravans numbering 1,600 to 2,000 slaves in the space of six weeks.

"The route traversed by these bands of slaves is strewed thick with skulls and human bones, and this horrifying statement can be fully confirmed by Messrs. Wilson and Felkin, who have only just passed over the same route.

"Surely it is time that we should cease to accept as true coin the evasions and excuses of the Khedive and his authorities. He should be given plainly to understand that England will no longer be put off with misstatements and subterfuges, and that as it has been proved that slave-hunting can be stopped — as it was when I was Governor of those countries — so it must now again be stopped.

"A decided message upon this point delivered by the English and French Governments would have a great effect. Something further ought, however, to be done by England, and I believe that the proper step for her to take would be the immediate appointment with full powers of a Consul for the Soudan, with a roving commission and headquarters at Khartoum, and with a salary of not less than £1,000 a year, as it would be necessary that he should not engage in any kind of trade.

"Another Consul for the Red Sea, with headquarters at Massowah, and a salary of £500 a year, should also be appointed to assist him.

"Copies of the Anglo-Egyptian Slave Convention, with the decree of 17th August, 1877, ought to be affixed to the doors of all Government offices in Cairo, and in all other places in Egypt and the Soudan, so that it should be seen and read by all the people.

"This Convention is full of grave faults and omissions, but still if carried out it would be better than nothing.

"In concluding this hurried review, I would only add that the time has now surely gone by for accepting false promises and paltry excuses. Let the Khedive and his people understand, without possibility of misunderstanding, that the Governments of England and France are now in earnest in their determination that this horrible scandal to humanity, this blot upon civilisation, shall at once and for ever be put an end to."

There is a note of weariness in one of Gordon's last letters, in G. B. Hill's *Colonel Gordon in Central Africa 1874-9*, London, 1881, pp. 348-9, before he left the Soudan. He is baffled by the scale of the slave trade.

When one thinks of the enormous numbers of slaves which have passed into Egypt from these parts in the last few years, one can scarcely conceive what has become of them and then again, where do they all come from? For the lands of the natives which I have seen are densely populated. We must have caught 2000 in less than nine months, and I expect we did not catch one-fifth of the caravans. Again how many died en route? The slaves are most undemonstrable. They make no signs of joy at being released. I suppose the long marches have taken all the life out of them.

Samuel Baker, who spent a year on the Sudan Abyssinian border during 1861-2, observed the flourishing state of the great slave mart at Gallabat on Abyssinia's northwestern border, from where large numbers of slaves were supplied to Egypt and Turkey. The following extract is from his *The Nile Tributaries of Abyssinia*, London, 1867, pp. 349-50.

On my return to camp I visited the establishments of the various slave merchants; these were arranged under large tents of matting, and contained many young girls of extreme beauty, ranging from nine to seventeen years of age. These lovely captives, of a rich brown tint, with delicately formed features, and eyes like those of the gazelle, were natives of the Galla, on the borders of Abyssinia, from which country they were brought by Abyssinian traders to be sold for the Turkish harems. Although beautiful, these girls were useless for hard labour; they quickly fade away and die unless kindly treated. They are the Venuses of that country, and not only are their faces and figures perfection, but they become extremely attached to those who show them kindness, and they make good and faithful wives. There is something peculiarly captivating in the natural grace and softness of those young beauties, whose hearts quickly respond to those warmer feelings of love and that are seldom known among the sterner and coarser tribes. Their forms are peculiarly elegant and graceful — the hands and feet are exquisitely delicate: the nose is slightly acquiline, the nostrils large and finely-shaped; the hair is black and glossy, reaching to about the middle of the back, but rather coarse in texture. These girls, although natives of Galla, invariably call themselves Abyssinians and are generally known under that denomination. They are exceedingly proud and high spirited and are remarkably quick at learning. At Khartoum several of the Europeans of high standing have married these charming ladies, who have invariably rewarded their husbands by great affection and devotion. The price of one of these beauties of Gallabat was from twenty-five to forty dollars.

M. Lucereau, a French traveller, writing from Zeila, on the African side of the Red Sea, on 6 July 1880, described the trade in slaves from that port. This extract appeared in the *Anti-Slavery Reporter*, Vol. 1, No. 4, May 1881.

The slaves are mostly Abyssinians and Adels, but above all the Galla prisoners of war. The Galla woman, the principal object of this trade, is a magnificent and sculpturesque creature, with an European profile (though some of them have slightly thick lips, and slightly prominent cheek bones). The skin is not black, but metallic and bronzed—veritable statues in Florentine Bronze. They fetch a great price, and are much prized by the Arabs, who superstitiously believe that a Galla woman can re-animate and renew the blood of an old man; and as the Arab only lives for his wife, and would ruin himself to have one, they always find purchasers at a high price.

The following account of the slave trade in the eastern Sudan is taken from '83 to '87 in the Soudan, London 1888, Vol. ii, pp. 242-66, by Mr A. B. Wylde, a 'roving consul', and son of the Head of the Slave Trade Department at the Foreign Office, Mr W. H. Wylde, who was also a member of the British and Foreign Anti-Slavery Society.

From the moment I took up my permanent residence in the Red Sea in the winter of 1874 and '75, I have probably had better opportunities of watching the workings of this demoralizing traffic than most people, and as it was always a labour of love to me catching a slave-dealer or annoying him in any way, I have spent many of my odd moments in trying to learn as much as possible about the trade with the view, when the time arrived, to be able to deal the traffic and all concerned in it a crushing blow. I feel strongly on the subject of slavery, and so would the most callous of fashionable English people if they knew all that took place. I want to enter into the argument of "Oh, the slave is much better off than if he were running about in his native country. Why should we interfere?" I agree altogether with this saying. The slave is better off on many occasions in captivity than when he is in his native country. Why should we interfere? For many reasons. For each slave that becomes happy (mind, after having passed through a lot of miseries before he gets to that state of happiness), statistics prove that at least ten people have died to bring the one slave into the so-called state of happiness and to pass his life as a sort of domestic beast of burden for an Arab master, sometimes below and sometimes a little above him in the social scale. Let the doctor dissect the slave and the master on death. With the exception of, if the slave is black, there is a different colouring in the skin, they are identically the same, member for member, and they are both the work of the Great God of Nature. The souls of both have not yet been dissected, so we are to take it for granted that they are the same.

The public would be very indignant if the black made a slave of the white, and for each white that was brought into captivity ten died. The traffic being associated with murder, fornication, rape, unsexing males, and every cruelty, therefore I dislike the traffic and those that participate in it, and I think it ought to be put down. Another reason, that as long as the slave trade goes on nominally under the protection of Turkey, no Christian merchant can well compete in the Soudan trade against the Mahommedan merchant, who buys the slave as a beast of burden, and it is only in cultivation where the Christian has the pull over the Moslem. Cultivation in the Soudan is a new industry, and it has not been possible to carry it on since the war broke out.

I think it better to work from Mecca and Jeddah back to where the slave comes from, as it is with the trade at Jeddah and the Soudan coast where I have been most brought into contact with it, and where I have learnt most of my experience. It must not be for one moment thought that all Arabs are slave-dealers; and there is a great deal of difference between the merchant that buys a slave or two for his own use and those that make their living out of it. There is a recognized slave market at Mecca, which is always more largely supplied during the pilgrimage than at any other time of year; and there are plenty of private markets at Jeddah where slaves are kept for sale, and where many of them are warehoused before being sent to Mecca.

The slave-brokers are a recognized guild both at Mecca and Jeddah; the slave merchants are all known, and there is hardly any secrecy, after one knows the country thoroughly, in how the whole business is conducted. Only at Jeddah, where there are European consuls, is there some show made by the Turks of preventing the slaves being exposed in public; but there is no difficulty in obtaining slaves at any time, and any Mahommedan is allowed to go and see those that are for sale.

Colonel Schaeffer, of the Egyptian service, was at Jeddah last year, and has made a report to Sir Evelyn Baring of what was going on there; the Egyptian officer attached to him had no difficulty in seeing the slaves for sale, and, I believe, was taken to see them by a Turkish military officer. Treaties with Turkey for the suppression of slavery are so much waste paper, as they have never been put in force properly. The Hedjaz may be said to be the ultimate destination of the majority of the African slaves, and from there they find their way to Turkey, Syria, and Persia, the great consuming centres for the inhabitants of poor Africa; it is for these people that the dark Continent must suffer, and the nameless miseries that are still going on must continue. The remedy is in the hands of England, and she has hitherto been the only champion of freedom. Happily for us Italy has now joined England in the Red Sea, and, as her traditions are against slavery, there seems to be every possibility of her being a most valuable ally in aiding to block the Red Sea passage. To Italy we have to look for help; France, the Republic, and the land of the most free, does not lift her little finger to put down slavery, and I do not think it can be recorded that she ever stopped a slaver or interested herself in putting down the East African slave trade.

The Hedjaz merchant, who is the most interested in the slave trade, is generally a man who is equivalent to our great employers of labour at home, and the slaves he buys he uses as carpenters, masons, coolies, boatmen, and divers (for the mother-o'-pearl trade). It is not because he cannot get other labour that he is forced to procure slaves at any price, but because the profits out of all these trades find their way into his pocket, and the only expenses he is put to is food and scanty clothing. The wage that ought to be paid, and which is so high in Christianized countries, and so cuts down the manufacturer to a small percentage on his capital, is here done away with. He fits out a caravan to go to the frontier markets of the Soudan, say such as Gallabat, Senaar, the Bahr el Gazelle provinces, or Darfur and Kordofan; there he has his agents, very often paid servants of his, who exchange the goods consigned forming the caravans, for slaves, out of which the whole of his profit is to be looked for; and here it is where the Hedjaz merchant has the pull over the Christian merchant or legitimate trader. His agents at these interior markets can purchase at a higher rate than others, all the high-priced and less bulky goods, such as gold dust, musk, ivory, and ostrich feathers, and get his slaves purchased to carry the goods to the coast, thereby saving transport, and the only camels he requires *en route* are a few to take water and food for the slaves.

With the Christian merchant at the interior market he has to content himself with gums, hides, drugs, and other large and weighty goods, which require many camels and hard labour to bring the produce down to the coast. Some of the slave-dealers at Jeddah and Suakim have, when competition has been brisk, contented themselves by taking up country only very light and valuable goods, such as silks, scents, etc., and then bought of the trader the commoner goods he has had all the trouble to bring up country, made use of that labour, and again bought his return caravans of slaves, and gone away in light marching order back to the coast. There can be no doubt who the inhabitants of the Soudan prefer, namely, the trader who brings them what they require, and pays high rates to them both backwards and forwards from the coast, to the man who only deals in slaves, from whom they make little or nothing out of. The slaves do not come from the country in which these carriers live, but far beyond their limits, and they would be only too glad to help the trader do away with the slaver; and the carrier, not being a slave raider, is not interested in slavery over and above purchasing one occasionally as a domestic slave. Very often this domestic slave is a girl, she gets married to a tribesman, or her master, perhaps, may get a child from her, and she immediately takes her place among the tribes, and is treated exactly the same as any of the other women.

The Hedjaz merchant does not content himself by buying just what he requires for his own use, but purchases all the slaves that he can get hold of—men, women, small children, young girls, young boys, and any eunuch that he can get hold of, they being always taken great care of and better fed, and allowed to ride nearly the whole way to the coast, as being more valuable. The women slaves, I need hardly say, are used for domestic purposes, and the Arab ladies in the Hedjaz prefer the ugliest they can get hold of, as there is less chance of their husbands being led astray. Woe betide the poor girl if she has anything like decent looks and the husband purchases her without the wife seeing her. Her life from the moment she enters the harem is made a burden to her, and many a "curtain lecture" takes place between husband and wife over the transaction. If the slave manages to get into the family way, and the husband thinks that he has every reason to believe that it is his fault, then the domestic slave gets better treated, but the wife always tries to make him believe that it is someone else. I have seen many of these cases, and the slave girls have come to me for protection, and I never knew a case hardly in which I was not able to arrange the matter amicably between master and slave, generally to the wife's disgust. The boys, according to their age, are used for different purposes. The first thing they are all done to is to undergo the rite of circumcision, and thereby made nominally Moslems. The small children are bought for household purposes, and generally brought up with the owner's children, if he has any. These small slaves are best off of all, and if they have a kind master and are intelligent it is their own fault often enough if they do not get on in the world; it, however, entirely depends on the caprice of the master. The boys that are large enough to commence learning a trade, as soon as they can get about after the operation they have undergone, are kept at work from sunrise to sunset, and it is astonishing how soon they pick up a trade and make themselves useful and a source of profit to their owners. Those that are turned into boatmen have hard work and get more abuse and kicks than the others. The most cruel work is the pearl diving; each boat may have two or three small slaves on board being taught how to dive. The plan is simple enough, after a few days' fishing, and when the boats are working over a mother-o'- pearl shell bank that may only have three or four fathoms over it, the small slaves are shown the shells that are brought up, and although perhaps they cannot swim, they are sent into the water—a stone tied to their feet, a loop placed under their arms, a basket tied around their waist, and down they are sent. At first off they are kept under water for about half-a-minute and then pulled up. If they have not picked up a shell or two they get the rope's end or the stick.

I know of no more sudden change for a small boy who has only just been introduced to the sea than being sent under water to get shells. It is impossible for him to escape, down he must go, on account of the heavy stone, and I often wondered what their feelings must be when first introduced to the depths of the sea. Many die from shock to the system and from fright, and when the living boy that went down is pulled up his owner finds that what was a slave is now only the shell of one, and that the poor little fellow knows the great secret. The life these poor little slaves lead till they become accustomed to the work is very hard. Other slaves are employed looking out after the flocks or in the date and fruit gardens, and their time is not such a hard one. The male slaves are entirely dependent on their owners if they are well treated or not; as with horses, some are well fed and treated, others are badly fed and not looked out after, and the master works them as hard as he can to make as much profit out of them in the shortest period possible. There is no society for the prevention of cruelty to animals or slaves in Arabia, and the lot of the animal or biped is a hard one, as there is only the slight moral sense of wrong that a living thing is being badly treated, and if they bring in the dollar it covers a multitude of sins, and is a sure salve to the conscience.

The African women slaves are used for domestic purposes, as it is only the poorest and most destitute of Arab women that will take service with other families. As long as an Arab woman is poor and has good looks she can always earn enough to live on, and she may make her way in the world by marriage or helping others to get married; therefore female slaves as servants are always in demand, not only in Arabia, but throughout the Mahommedan world. Of course the women slaves most thought of and in the greatest demand are the Abyssinians, who are liked for their superior talents, and they are very often taken great care of. The traffic in true Abyssinians is nearly unknown, and those that find their way into the market have generally been kidnapped at the Soudan frontier towns. The Galla girls are also called Abyssinians, but there is a difference between the two. The Gallas can be got in great numbers, and there is little known of their country.

It is quite wrong to accuse either King John or King Menelek of having anything to do with the slave trade, as the Mahommedans capture and purchase the Gallas from the far west and south and east of the Galla country. They hold the unenviable position of being surrounded on three sides by slave hunters, and till now we have had no chance of getting among the Gallas and making friends with them. If the men of this country are anything like their women, they will stand a great chance of taking the highest position amongst the tribes of Africa. The women are very pretty, have good figures, small hands and feet, soon become most cleanly in their person and dress, pick up all the benefits of civilization, get fairly educated, make good servants, and are faithful and loveable. They show no signs of negro origin, either as regards hair or features, and they are nearly all of them a light brown colour, the brown getting lighter according to altitude above the sea. The mother of many an Egyptian or Turk in high position has hailed from the Galla country or Abyssinia.

A great many of the eunuchs sold in Mecca come originally from the Galla country; it is, of course, hard to trace exactly where these poor children are operated on, but there can be no doubt that some of them are made so at or near Hodeidah, actually unsexed in a country flying a flag recognized by all the European nations, and a nation we are all led to believe ought to have the same status as other civilized powers.

Turkey only purchases black and brown eunuchs because she cannot procure others. If she had her way and had the chance, she might buy white ones. What a howl there would be by the mothers in England, and how scandalized they would be if a Turkish vessel came off Brighton or some other watering-place and took away a boat-load or two of the surplus male children that play about on the beach, to be manufactured into harem guards. It is done within less than ten days of London now, and a time may come when the Turk could again do the same in Europe. The black and brown eunuchs are generally made in the interior, at the different slave stations. The smallest boys that are hardly worth their keep for six months, are taken *en masse* and operated upon, and those that live become very valuable and are taken care of, as they then fetch high prices, not only in the country, but at their destination, wherever it may be — Hodeidah, Jeddah, or Cairo.

There are three sorts of eunuchs. The description of the operation is not fit for publication, but the commonest kind is where everything is removed. On my last voyage home from Jedda, *viâ* Tangiers, there were three eunuchs on board taken as a present for the Sultan of Morocco. Their ages averaged from eight to twelve, the oldest being a very pretty Galla boy. They had only just been operated on, and gave an intelligent account of what they had undergone. Their case was reported at Tor, the quarantine station, to the Egyptian authorities, and again to the Governor at Suez, but no steps were taken to punish those that had the eunuchs with them. Besides being used as harem guards, the better-looking Galla eunuchs are used for immoral purposes.

I will believe the Egyptians and Turks are sincere in their endeavours to put down the slave trade when they cease to allow eunuchs to appear in public, and when they are not the occupants of the carriage boxes when a pasha's lady takes her afternoon drive. All eunuchs ought to be registered, what number exist now known, and any person in future purchasing a eunuch or found with one in his possession under the age of ten years to be immediately punished and the eunuch confiscated and placed in a hospital for incurables. If eunuchs are so essential to the life of the higher classes of Egypt and Turkey they ought to have them manufactured from their own sons. Let it be given out that Achmed or Abdullah has renounced the pleasures of this world and has sacrificed himself for the good of his family, and that will hereafter attend on his father's wives and concubines. The manufacture of eunuchs is the most revolting part of the many horrors of the slave trade, and no one but a few Englishmen seem to stir to denounce it. Our treaties with Turkey are so much waste paper, and the Turkish pasha chuckles at what he does, and buys his eunuch or slave whenever he requires one in spite of all treaties and all promises. I have never seen a eunuch among the Eastern Soudan tribesmen, so they do not make the demand. If the Turkish and Egyptian pasha did not buy the eunuch there would be no demand, consequently no supply.

How many years more is this to be allowed to continue, and how many lives have there been sacrificed for the eunuchs that are seen on the Shoubra road any Friday afternoon? Every one of them represent at the very least 200 Soudanese done to death to satisfy the requirements of the wealthy class at Cairo and elsewhere. Say there are 500 eunuchs in Cairo to-day, 100,000 Soudanese have died to procure these eunuchs; there is no exaggeration in what I am saying, and how can any Egyptian official that owns one be sincere when he is partly the cause of this misery? He may be, perhaps, a minister, and in communication with our representative regarding the suppression of the slave trade. What reliance can be placed on what he says? Simply none. It was the same with the Sultan of Zanzibar; certainly his treaty putting down the traffic in slaves was a step in the right direction, but it was not enough, and as long as he held slaves, and eunuchs were about his establishment, the other Arabs could see that he evaded the treaty, and if he could they would do so as well.

The great question becomes, What is to be done to put a stop to this vile trade that is depopulating Africa and causing so much misery to millions of human beings? England's list of brave sons that have died in their attempt to put an end to slavery and to open up Africa will increase unless the present treaties are put into force and we demand our rights under them. The Egyptian is now by force obliged to do something, as he is looked out after. There is no reason no doubt that the moment the last English soldier leaves Egypt that the influence of our representative there will cease, and the slave trade will commence again afresh. This will open the northern roads. The eastern roads, pointing from the interior of the Soudan towards Mecca and Hodeidah, are in full swing, and a great trade is being done. We have the most lamentable accounts of the increased Arab activity and the slave trade from the interior round the lakes, to what may be called the Zanzibar or Equatorial coast. Westward, one may say, the slave trade has entirely ceased, northward to Morocco, Algeria, Tunis, Tripoli, and Egypt it still goes on, but from all accounts in Egypt, Tunis, and Algeria to a lesser extent than to Morocco and Tripoli. The only evidence I can get regarding the northern slave trade is what I have from residents, and from what I read, regarding the Zanzibar and Equatorial littoral as well, but from Suez down to the Red Sea from personal experience. I shall, therefore, confine my remarks to the latter.

There can be no doubt that the increased Arab activity all over eastern Africa is due greatly to what has been done in the Soudan, and it is the final great Arab struggle whether Africa is to be left to them commercially with its concomitant horrors of the slave trade, and depopulation, or that civilized commerce, cultivation, and the opening up of the country is to take place, and that the European is to help the black central races against the Arab and his slave-dealing friends. I have no doubt in my mind what the result will be, and that it will be a decided victory for the European and black as soon as the former can help the latter, and teach him to defend himself, which may be done in many ways. Instead of looking on with concern at what the Germans, Italians, and Belgians are doing in Africa, we ought to hail with delight the help these free countries will give us. I do not wish it to be understood that we are to fold our hands and allow them to cut us out, but, that instead of neglecting our interests, go on defining them when any question arises so that we make a friendly march forward to the interior in the great work of civilization and Christianizing the black, if he is willing to become Christianized. The slave trade question in the Red Sea is not the complicated one which most people think it. Those Europeans that have had a long residence are willing to give their experience, so any naval officer new to the business can always get information if he is not too proud to ask for it.

I do not know if the Admiralty bureaucracy publish any hints or information for commanders going to the Red Sea slave cruising, but they might do so and simplify matters. It depends more on the Admiralty by supplying proper ships than anything else, and it is no use and only heart-breaking work for a commander to be sent down to the Red Sea cruising and to have charge of a steamer that will neither sail properly nor steam, unless there is a dead calm, and that he knows is not fast enough to keep up with an ordinary native boat. How many slavers have escaped through this, and many of the owners of the dhows as long as there is a steady north wind blowing laugh at the cruisers on the station, as they are so slow. If the public think that the men-of-war sent to the Red Sea are up to their work they are greatly mistaken; officers and men are, but the ships and boats are not.

One of our cruisers was towed out of the Red Sea during '84-'85 three times as she could not steam against a headwind. Our blockade of the coast for the suppression of the slave trade has been and is now a farce. There is no Intelligence Department and absolutely no sum of money at the disposal of either the Consul or the naval officers to procure information. There has been a few captures made of boats coming across from Jeddah to take slaves back, and in ten years or more the actual captures of dhows with slave cargoes on board can be counted on the fingers of one hand: not one boat, perhaps, in a thousand has been caught, and when these captures have been made it has been from evidence obtained on shore. What ought to be served out to every officer on the station is a map with the slave routes from the interior, the boat harbours, the wells along the coast, and every information that might prove of use, and a sum of money put at the disposal of the Consul and the senior naval officer for procuring evidence, but only remuneration paid when a capture takes place, or when it was not the fault of the informant that the dhow escaped. It is generally known when slaves are *en route* to the coast; all the tribesmen know the slavers' hiding places, and they make nothing out of the slave-dealers. While the tribesmen had to depend on the slave-dealers for their supplies, which they had to do greatly since 1884, they, of course, could not be expected to give information against those that fed them, but when the tribal ports are opened to commerce there can be no doubt that the tribesmen will be willing to help their true friends, the merchants, to put a stop to the transactions of the enemies of both. I do not think that the tribesmen will say, "Let us have both the slave-dealer and the merchant at our ports so as we can play the one off against the other and get our manufactures cheaper," for what with competition there is no chance of a monopoly at any port, so the merchant cannot dictate his terms to the tribes.

I do not wish for one moment that anyone who reads this should think that I am finding fault and saying unpleasant things just for the sake of making myself disagreeable, but there has been lately a certain amount of neglect shown in dealing with the slave trade which is not creditable to Englishmen. I don't for one moment wish to attribute any fault to the officers and men that have had the hard work of cruising in one of the hottest climates in the world, and I sympathize with them in all their difficulties. The fault can be traced to the Admiralty for sending and fitting out ships for the station totally useless for the purpose for which they are employed.

If these class of gunboats are not fast enough for slave cruising they are not fast enough to protect our commerce, and I am afraid that the whole of our older gunboats and sloops are only of use in peace time to carry the English flag about, and it is very doubtful if war broke out whether they could get into places of safety in time before many of them were captured. We have many thousands of fighting men in these obsolete ships with their obsolete armaments, and one-quarter of the number of modern gunboats would do the work they do. I don't say that there ought to be only a quarter of the number, but it would be more businesslike to have a few good boats than a lot of bad ones.

Fast ships are required, vessels that can steam, not hold their way against a head wind, and not a naval officer will say that craft like the *Falcon, Condor, Gannet, Cygnet, Dolphin, Coquette, Albacore, Bittern, Beacon, Decoy*, &c., &c., and this class of sloop or gun boat that have been employed lately in the Red Sea, are fit to cope with their work. Some of them can do with difficulty ten knots in a calm, but as the usual Red Sea weather is not what may be called calm, and the wind is either blowing strongly from the north or south, the progress these cruisers make through the water is, average them all round, about five knots. This speed is not enough, and until a faster type of cruisers is used few captures will be made. The naval officer can only be expected to do his duty, and I have heard complaints from nearly every commander of this tenor: "What is the use of sending us here to stop the slave trade? You first put us in vessels that won't steam, you won't aid us to get information, and if we make a mistake and arrest a vessel and we cannot prove slavery against her, we are liable to prosecution for illegal detention, and it is the servant of the nation, and not the nation, that has to pay the damages."

The great mistake that all commanders of cruisers make is that they keep too near and in sight of the Soudan shore of the Red Sea. A man-of-war is a most conspicuous mark and can be seen for miles, and the natives that are engaged in the slave trade have a very perfect system of signals and information, and they generally know the whereabouts and movements of every one of Her Majesty's ships and if they are fast or slow. It is needless to say the head quarters of this espionage is at Suakim; it used to be before the war in Jeddah.

The question of catching slaves becomes a game of skill played between the senior naval officer and the traders. With reliable information and quick cruisers the advantage is all on the side of the naval officers. Now everything is in favour of the others, and so it will be, and no blow can be struck until the public insist on proper ships being sent out, and that they will not grudge the two or three thousand pounds per annum that it will cost to procure the information that will lead to the increased captures.

There is, if one takes a look at the map of the Red Ṣea, more chance of making captures off Jeddah and on the south of Hodeidah (where the southern dhows make for) than by cruising off the long bit of coast from Mersa Halaib to Zeilah; and it is not likely that the slave-dealers for some time will use the other ports on the Hedjaz or Arabian side; certainly not until they receive a severe blow by losing a good many dhows, laden with slaves, and then when they alter their routes and the British public will allow information to be paid for, they can again be checkmated by our cruisers.

One slave-dealer hanged for slavery on the coast will do more good than fifty captures, and I wish it to be understood that until a rough and ready justice is meted out to these lawless people no permanent good can be expected. What did Gordon do in the Soudan? I take a couple of his letters to me: —

"Khartoum,
"19 — 8 — 1878.

"MY DEAR WYLDE,

"Thanks for your letter of the 5th August, and the papers, which are very interesting. I have telegraphed about the subsidy to the steamer, and thanks for sending the dhurra. Mind and let me know if you have the slightest bother with Redwan or Aboubekr, Pashas at Berberah and Zeilah, but be just with them and do not take advantage of our friendship. I will walk into them, you may be sure, if they *attempt* to thwart you or your people, for I am extremely angry with Redwan Pasha.

"I have hung one man in Obeid for mutilating a boy, and hope to hang five more in a couple of days. We have caught 17 caravans in three months, and I am now trying to catch a sandjak who, with 80 men, was conveying 400 slaves from Darfur. Rossit met him *en route* and ordered him to stop. He refused and threatened to fire on him. If I catch him I will hang him.

> "Believe me,
> > "My dear Wylde,
> > > "Yours sincerely,
> > > > "C. G. GORDON."

The dhurra was sent by me to Berberah and Zeilah for Colonel Gordon, as there was a famine there, and Redwan and Aboubekr Pashas had turned corn merchants like Joseph did in Pharaoh's time. The grain arrived unexpectedly at these places and the market fell a hundred per cent., much to the disgust of the Pashas and delight of the people. After the lesson there were no more "rings" started at the expense of the inhabitants. Rossit died on his way to the Sobat, where he and Gessi with a small force were going to try and open up this river and make friends with the Galla people. The expedition did not take place, as Gessi had to go to Darfur to suppress Suleiman Zebehr's insurrection. The sandjak, who was a governor of one of Gordon's districts in Darfur, was caught, tried by a court martial in Khartoum, and hanged.

> "Shaka Darfur,
> > "23rd April, 1879.

"MY DEAR WYLDE,

"Thanks for your kind note, its enclosure from Playfair, and the seeds (cinchona),* which will be sown in Khartoum. Thanks also for sending the £1,000 and for the dhurra. You never let me know how much I owe you for it. You will hear of the clean sweep made at Cairo of the whole lot. I heard of it last night by telegraph from Cairo, and am heartily glad of it, for the whole gang were an unpractical, square-headed set, with their European ideas and continual importations of new men. What a lot of money that man — —has cost H.H. Why, all these new men will have to be paid off a nice legacy he leaves. However, his light as a financier is out. Your father has never answered my letters; I expect he got them. Gessi has, after eight engagements, routed the revolted slave-dealers, and I hope hourly to hear of the capture and death of the leaders. He has had some heavy fighting. I am rooting them out of these lands; we have caught 71 caravans since June, 1878. If things do not get altered you must try and put a steamer on for Berberah, and (without a longer contract than three months) for £150 a month. I cannot offer with safety a longer time or more money.

> "Yours sincerely,
> > "C. G. GORDON."

* Eucalyptus.

I used to hear from time to time from Colonel Gordon about the slave trade, but where, I may say, I was in such constant communication with him was by telegraph; and many an evening I have spent in the telegraph station, he at one end of the line and I at the other, talking through the clerks on all sorts of subjects. There has not been the chance before nor since to deal with the slave trade as there is at present; but if the Admiralty and the Foreign Office will do their duty there is no reason why in a measurable time the slave trade should not cease to exist. The public must not for one moment think that they are not the volunteers and people who are capable of dealing with the slave-dealers. It is the bonds of red tape — in some cases worse than slave-irons — that prevent action being taken; and there can be but one ending to the question if the Government will only help the merchant, viz., the overthrow of the slave-dealers. The Government need only see that the treaties now made and in their keeping are carried out, send an extra cruiser in the Red Sea besides the three now there, and let these cruisers be vessels that can steam, instead of the Noah's arks that now do duty.

It is an insult to common sense the way things are being done at present, and no one knows it better than those who have to do the work. The merchant will help to get rid of the slave-dealer, as true trade and slavery can never live side by side. The population of Africa that is being gradually diminished year by year are the people to which the merchants will have to look to purchase their goods. As soon as the merchant can get among the blacks he can help them to protect themselves against the Arab slave-dealers; and with the blacks resisting the raids, and the cruisers, by the aid of an Intelligence Department, capturing the slave-dealers with their slaves just as they are reaching their final destination, will soon make slavery impossible.

As I have said before, the tribes of the Eastern Soudan will, if asked, be glad to help in putting down slavery; and now Italy has Massowah the task becomes easier, as part of the coast is held by a Christian nation. It will be a good thing for humanity at large when the rest of the Soudan coast falls into the hands of another civilized power. The time is now or never to get something done. Russia having taken a great part of the country from which Turkey drew her white slaves, blacks or browns will be more sought after to fill the harems and to do the domestic work; and it will be better at once to insist upon Turkey performing what she has bound herself to do than to allow her to go until she says, "If you will do something else for me, give in on such a point, I will see that the importation of slaves is really put a stop to." With Turkey, I am afraid, we have always made concessions and gone on half-hearted measures, instead of seeing that she carries out, not her promises, but what she has agreed to in writing. With what our politicians have done in the Soudan it is very much like the kettle calling the pot black, when we ask Turkey to do justice to the African, but there is no reason why the public should not insist on our Foreign Office doing their duty. I do not think that we grumble enough about the details and general management of the great public questions. There is, thank God, a feeling at last that our house is not in order, and a wholesome attempt being made to put our naval and military portions of the construction somewhat into a proper working condition. The public are grumbling that they are not getting their money's worth, and we certainly do not get the information we ought from the Civil Service, who I have nothing to say against individually, although they, on the whole, cannot be congratulated on the work they carry out. A leaf might be taken out of the American Consular Service and their example followed. I am sorry that they have not a Consul in the Red Sea to help in putting down the slave trade; we should then see the Turk wake up and try to do his duty. Our Consuls in the Red Sea, with the brilliant exception of poor Consul Moncrieff, have been mostly of the fossil order, and as the majority of their work is slave work and with the navy, it is a pity that naval officers are not appointed to these posts at Suakim and Jeddah. Their appointment to these posts would be a step in the right direction, especially if men were chosen that had some experience of the slave trade. Let them have fast cruisers to work with, and the public would see a very different result from what there is at present. There is always the question, What is to be done with the slaves when they are caught? The moment the country quiets down it is to be hoped that we will have a branch of the Universities Mission started at Suakim who will undertake a simple education and teaching the slaves some trade. The Barca Delta will take as many slaves as are caught. There will be no difficulty in getting them remunerative employment working in the cotton fields; they can be employed by the naval forces as stokers and doing cleaning work on board as at present. The police and army will always take some, and there is no reason why when the time comes that they may not return to the interior, and with the discipline that they have undergone, and their having mixed with civilization, they will be able to tell their own countrymen that the European is their friend and will help them against the Arab. The black soon begins to believe in the universal God, and to know the difference between right and wrong. This is enough Christianity for him as a commencement. There are now many hundreds of Bongos, Shilloks, Denkas, and other tribesmen in the Egyptian army. Some of them are most intelligent and are good soldiers. The moment these people get back to their homes they would have the rest of their tribesmen with them, and they could laugh at the slave-dealers as they could make no more raids on their country. I have great hopes that the slaves that have been torn from their homes under Egyptian rule will help in the future to pacify the Soudan and put an end to the slave-dealers. General Gordon, before he left the Soudan, had settled many of the captured slaves down in fertile parts of the country, and it was astonishing what advancement they were making. His successor broke up these colonies, and the people were made slaves again, There is no reason why the tribal people at Tokar should quarrel with any colonies started in the delta, as there is room there for all, and it has always been a district in which all the tribesmen had rights of pasturage and met on a peaceful footing, and the slave-colony would help the sheiks in clearing the land for cultivation. It is from an ignorance of Arab customs that the Tokar question has been so misjudged by the present Governor-General at Suakim, and he has been guided by what the Suakim people and the slave-dealers say, who are interested parties, and would like to have the whole management of the delta, which they will never get unless the English Government kills off all its inhabitants, which is not likely.

We have now on the Eastern Soudan littoral the following elements to work against the slave trade, and it only wants our Government (or, more strictly speaking, the Foreign Office that governs our Government, no matter to what party it belongs) to say "Trade shall be opened, and we will see that slave-dealing Arabs are punished when cases have been proved against them." The moment the Foreign Office says trade shall be opened the European merchant takes the place of the Arab slave-dealing merchant from Jeddah, and the tribesmen are brought into contact with civilization and legitimate trade, and people that will help him to develop the resources of his country instead of keeping him in ignorance and darkness. We have the Italians, who will be glad to help in opening Africa, and will, no doubt, by defining what they require, have no cause to be jealous of English merchants who are at one with them in wishing to see peace and prosperity, as against war and its devastations and misery. We have King John, who will, from what I know of him, welcome the merchant and the capitalist to trade with his country as long as the merchant confines himself to his legitimate calling and does not seek to alter the religion of his subjects and to intrigue with them.

Abyssinia is the coming country of Africa, with its splendid climate and mineral, natural, and agricultural riches, and its inhabitants with whom it is possible to associate, and are capable of great development. Then there is the Somali country, of which little is known, but its people have a liking for the English, and the Aden Government is looked up to by them all. Lastly, between the Somali country and Zanzibar, there is a new company starting, to which everyone ought to wish success; and there can be no doubt that it has a brilliant future before it if properly managed. It would be a great thing for Africa if Zanzibar could be dealt with and handed over to a civilized power, as the Arab's civilization will never deal with the mainland in a proper manner, and as long as it is in the hands of the Arabs they will always foster the slave trade in one way or another.

Brave Emin Bey, as long as he lives, will form a point round which civilization should rally; and he is a bright example of what one foreigner unaided can accomplish. England's, Italy's, and King John's subjects at peace with the tribesmen would soon settle the Soudan question, and that of the slave trade; but as long as there is no action taken against the purchasers of slaves and those that foster the trade, so long will there be victims to the cause of civilization and liberty. We have had enough horrors in the Soudan to satisfy everyone; let us have a new departure and finish once and for all the wicked idea of trying to reconquer the Soudan for Egypt, or allowing the military to keep up the policy that is now being carried on, which only tends towards bloodshed. Egypt's best neighbour is a friendly Soudan; they cannot reconquer it by force of arms, but it is to be re-conquered by trade, and its inhabitants are to be made friendly, and will themselves deal with Mahdism and the slave trade as long as they know they are not to be handed back to the hated Egyptian rule. It is impossible for the English military officer as long as he puts the tarbush on his head to talk to the tribesmen. He, therefore, stands on his dignity, and gets angry if a civilian tries to step in between and bring about a reconciliation. What England refuses to do for civilization and commerce, Italy will not only be too glad to perform, and, before long, British merchants will make overtures to Italians to help them settle a question which is rightly England's duty to see carried out.

There are no responsibilities that can follow by dealing honestly with the Soudan and confining English interests to the coast; complications are likely to arise by neglecting and failing to deal with the question in a manly and straightforward manner. In God's name let us have a settlement of the question, and try to make some reparation for the amount of blood-guiltiness we have on our hands, and by our future behaviour strive to wash away the stain that disgraces the name of England in her dealings with the Soudan during the last few years.

THE SLAVE TRADE OF EASTERN AFRICA WITH
THE MIDDLE EAST COUNTRIES

Any account of the slave trade of Eastern Africa with the Middle East must include the slave trade in white slaves, especially with Turkey. This extract is taken from Edmund Spencer's *Travels in Circassia,* London, 1839, p. 157.

Circassians, Georgians, and Grecians were the most valued and always estimated according to their beauty. The two former being very difficult to procure, on account of the strict blockade maintained by Russia on the Circassian coast of the Black Sea, now fetch as high a price as a hundred pounds; a well-made healthy Abyssinian might be purchased for about thirty, while the poor negro woman was not considered worth more than ten or fifteen.

As late as 1910, Ella C. Sykes, in *Persia and its People,* New York, 1910, p. 69, speaks of negresses being expensive slaves in Persia, 'though many are still being introduced by pilgrims from Mecca'.
And according to a report at the mid-nineteenth century from Consul-General Bruce to Lord Stratford,

Black slaves and black eunuchs form an essential part of the establishment of every rich Turk, and they are supplied exclusively from the regions that border the upper Nile, every attempt will be made to render inoperative the measures taken by Said Pasha for the abolition of the traffic.

SP LXIV 1857, No 592, Cairo, 1 January 1855.

The following extract is taken from the *Anti-Slavery Reporter,* Vol. IV, Third Series, 1 September 1856.

SLAVERY IN TURKEY

In the April number of the *Reporter* we published an address on Turkish Slavery and the slave-trade, which the Committee of the *British and Foreign Anti-Slavery Society* had presented, early in the previous month, to Viscount Palmerston, with a view that the subject thereof should be brought under the notice of the Peace Conference then sitting at Paris. In the article which preceded this Address, we set forth at some length the peculiar reasons which, in our judgment, existed for the interference of the representatives of the Christian Powers to put an end to the purchase and sale of Circassian and Georgian slaves, apart altogether from the broad principles on which we urged Her Majesty's Government to use its influence for the suppression of the slave-trade generally, and of Slavery throughout the Turkish dominions. We have reason to believe that the attention of Her Majesty's Minister for Foreign Affairs is directed to this subject, of which we ourselves shall not lose sight. Meanwhile, the nature, extent, and consequence of the system of Slavery existing in Turkey, and which the *Times* of the 1st of March last unblushingly apologized for, may be judged of from the subjoined communication, from the Constantinople correspondent of the *Morning Post*, published in a recent number of this journal.

"There has been lately an unusually large number of Circassians going about the streets of Constantinople. Many of them, no doubt, belonged to the deputation which came to petition the Porte that their country might be taken under the suzerainty of the Sultan – an arrangement which, of course, was inadmissible under the late treaty of peace. Before the war it was a disputed point whether or not Russia had a right, by any treaty with Turkey, to overrun Circassia; now, however, her claim has been, in a manner, tacitly recognized. But, *de facto*, nothing is changed, for Russia will now have no more power over the mountain tribes than she can obtain by arms, and that was the state of things before as well as during the war. It was perhaps fortunate that Mr. Longworth's mission accomplished nothing in the way of securing the Circassians as active allies in the late campaigns, for it is probable enough that we should have been obliged to sacrifice them at last, especially as our allies took no part in the mission to the Caucasus.

"A considerable portion, however, of the Circassians now in the capital have quite another mission than a political one to fulfil. They are here as slave-dealers, charged with the disposal of the numerous parcels of Circassian girls that have been for some time pouring into this market. Perceiving that when the Russians shall have re-occupied the coast of the Caucasus this traffic in white slaves will be over, the Circassian dealers have redoubled their efforts ever since the commencement of the Peace Conferences to introduce into Turkey the greatest possible number of women while the opportunity of so doing lasted. They have been so successful, notwithstanding the prohibition of the trade by the Porte, and the presence of so many of her Majesty's ships in the Black Sea, that never, perhaps, at any former period, was white human flesh so cheap as it is at this moment. There is an absolute glut in the market, and dealers are obliged to throw away their goods, owing to the extent of the supply, which, in many instances, has been brought by steam under the British flag. In former times a 'good middling' Circassian girl was thought very cheap at 100*l*., but at the present moment the same description of goods may be had for 5*l*.! In fact, the creatures are eating their heads off, and must be disposed of at any sacrifice, however alarming.

"Independently of all political, humane, and Christian objections to this abominable state of things, there are several practical ones which have even forced themselves on the attention of the Turks. With low prices a low class of purchasers come into the market. Formerly a Circassian slave-girl was pretty sure of being bought into a good family, where not only good treatment, but often rank and fortune awaited her; but at present low rates she may be taken by any huxter, who never thought of keeping a slave before. Another evil is, that the temptation to possess a Circassian girl at such a low price is so great in the minds of the Turks, that many who cannot afford to keep several slaves have been sending their blacks to market in order to make room for a newly-purchased white girl. The consequence is, that numbers of black women, after being as many as eight or ten years in the same hands, have lately been consigned to the broker for disposal. Not a few of those wretched creatures are in a state quite unfit for being sold. I have it on the authority of a respectable slave-broker, that at the present moment there have been thrown on the market unusually large numbers of negresses in the family-way, some of them even slaves of pachas and men of rank. He finds them so unsaleable, that he has been obliged to decline receiving any more. A single observation will explain the reason of this, which might appear strange when compared with the value that is attached even to an unborn black baby in some slave countries. In Constantinople it is evident that there is a very large number of negresses living and having habitual intercourse with their Turkish masters, yet it is a rare thing to see a mulatto. What becomes of the progeny of such inter-course? I have no hesitation in saying that it is got rid of by infanticide, and that there is hardly a family in Stamboul where infanticide is not practiced in such cases as a mere matter of course, and without the least remorse or dread."

T. E. Lawrence, travelling north from Rabegh on the Red Sea in World War I, visited slave villages in Wadi Safra, and described them in *Seven Pillars of Wisdom*, London, 1926, p. 89.

At the most, the tribal Arabs of Wadi Safra lived in their villages five months a year. For the other seasons the gardens were entrusted to slaves, negroes like the grown lads who brought in the tray to us, and whose thick limbs and plump shining bodies looked curiously out of place among the bird-like Arabs. Khallaf told me these blacks were originally from Africa, brought over as children by their nominal Takruri fathers, and sold during the pilgrimage, in Mecca. When grown strong they were worth from fifty to eighty pounds a piece, and were looked after carefully as befitted their price. Some became house or body servants with their masters; but the majority were sent out to the palm villages of these feverish valleys of running water, whose climate was too bad for Arab labour, but where they flourished and built themselves solid houses, and mated with women slaves, and did all the manual work of the holding.

They were very numerous—for instance, there were thirteen villages of them side by side in this Wadi Safra—so they formed a society of their own, and lived much at their pleasure. Their work was hard, but the supervision loose, and escape easy. Their legal status was bad, for they had no appeal to tribal justice, or even to the Sherif's courts; but public opinion and self interest deprecated any cruelty towards them, and the tenet of the faith that to enlarge a slave is a good deed, meant in practice that nearly all gained freedom in the end. They made pocket-money during their service, if they were ingenious. Those I saw had property and declared themselves contented. They grew melons, marrows, cucumbers, grapes, and tobacco for their own account, in addition to the dates, whose surplus was sent across to the Sudan by sailing dhow, and there exchanged for corn, clothing and the luxuries of Africa and Europe.

The *Anti-Slavery Reporter*, Vol VI, Fourth Series, October and November, 1886, published a copy of a letter from a young officer cruising in the Persian Gulf, dated 10 September 1886.

Slavery hereabouts is a dreadful thing, and it is a disgrace to the civilised countries of Europe that it should go on. England alone takes any steps in the matter, and those are only half measures, as only three ships are employed on the whole of the South and East Coasts of Arabia, and three more on the East Coast of Africa and Madagascar, which is absurdly insufficient to stop the traffic. Some of the domestic Slaves appear to be fairly well treated, and look comfortable, although, of course, they have all the hard work to do. Others are very cruelly treated. Perhaps the worst part of the whole thing is the pearl-diving. The strongest Slaves are chosen for this, and before they dive for the pearl oysters a clip is put on their nose to prevent their breathing. They then jump out of the boat, armed with a hammer and a light basket, and on coming to the surface pass the oysters into the boat, and after a whiff of air are sent down again. If they don't succeed in sending up a certain number of oysters they get severely beaten. Before long their lungs begin to give way, and then it is soon all over with them. I often think that if some ladies who wear pearls ever knew what it cost to get them they would chuck them out of the window to the first beggar they saw."

V

THE NAVAL ANTI-SLAVE TRADE
PATROL

The vast extent of waters and shoreline over which the British naval anti-slave trade patrol kept watch, from Mozambique in the south to the Baluchistan coast in the north, posed a formidable task for the slender patrol of from three to seven ships assigned to it. It was made more difficult by the increasing use of the French flag by Arab slavers, for under it they had immunity from search and capture by British cruisers.

The sea craft, the Indian Ocean dhow, which conveyed thousands of slaves from the East African coast to the Middle East, is described by Captain Owen in his *Narrative* Vol. 1, p. 384, on his survey of the coast in 1822-4:

their extraordinary construction did not fail to attract our attention. They are generally sixty feet long by about fourteen broad, their stem terminating in a long sharp point, with a lofty and overhanging stern; and as they are built like a wedge, upon grounding they are obliged to be kept in a perpendicular position, by means of small wooden shores which they always carry for the purpose. Their planking is more frequently secured to the ribs by coir lashings than by either nails or bolts, and in some the seats or beams project a short distance through the side, like the boats of Delagoa and the Massula boats of Madras. Their huge square sail of canvas or matting, has a yard above and one below, with braces and three or four bow-lines; yet, notwithstanding their uncouth appearance, they are always well manned, and generally pull with sixteen oars or paddles, excepting in shoal water, when they are propelled by means of long slender poles used against the ground, in the management of which the natives are very dextrous. These dhows have sometimes a small canopied space near the stern, on which, when prosecuting their voyage, the turbaned old chief, or master, may often be seen issuing his commands. They scarcely ever use iron anchors, their usual custom being to make them formed of wood, with four arms like a grapnel, and the inside of the shank loaded with heavy stones."

Captains G. L. Sulivan and P. Colomb, two young British naval officers employed on the naval anti-slave trade patrol at the mid-century, recount the thrill of the chase, and the frustration and difficulty in pursuing their task of suppressing the slave trade at sea. Always facing them is the ineluctable fact that until the Sultan of Zanzibar declares against it, their efforts are in vain.

Captain Sulivan outlines in *Dhow Chasing in Zanzibar Waters*, London 1873, pp. 58-63 and pp. 115-16, the nature of the East African slave trade, and the difficulties faced in distinguishing its legal and illegal aspects.

THERE are three distinct forms of this trade, which may be classed under the following heads: —

1. The illegal slave-trade;
2. The legal slave-trade; and
3. The so-called "LEGAL TRADER'S" slave-trade.

Of the two former we shall speak hereafter. It was the last we had most to do with here, because we were south of Cape Delgado, which is the southern limit of the dominions of the Sultan of Zanzibar (or of the Imaum of Muscat as he was then), and therefore no slave-trade was legal where we were.

The "legal trader's slave-trade" sounds paradoxical, but though it always appears to have existed, it is only latterly that there has been any attempt to recognize it, within certain limits, as a legal proceeding, and yet it is by far the most extensive of the three. As regards the two former there can never be any dispute.

By "legal trader's slave-trade" is meant that trade carried on in the coasting dhows which are engaged legally in conveying the produce of the country: ivory, copal, hides, rice, and corn, and in illegally smuggling a few slaves on board, or as many as they can stow conveniently with the least possible risk, but which have no licence or authority for conveying them even in Zanzibar territory, where it is possible to obtain such licences. The negoda (i.e. captain), whether he be owner or not, purchases a few slaves at the first port he puts into, and increases their number at each port as he proceeds north, until, as the dhow nears the destination it is finally bound for, where the inconvenience will be felt but for a short time longer and the risk of capture is almost "nil", she has become filled with slaves stowed in all manner of ways, and unless the cargo is such as they can be fed from, they are in a starving condition.

A common practice exists amongst Arab passengers in these dhows to pay the negoda for their voyage by bringing a slave with them from the shore, the proceeds of whose sale at a northern market yields the passage-money; it is just such cases as this that have been made use of by some persons to prove that dhows have been captured with only domestic slaves on board, and such cases are the most difficult of proof, because the Arabs, who know full well the English view and meaning of "domestic slaves," will swear that they are such. Such a case was that, no doubt, brought before the Select Committee, — I allude to the case of the "Petrel," which captured a dhow with Arab passengers on board, and six wretched creatures, whom the Arabs declared were "domestic slaves," as they will say and swear anything to deceive the authorities and gain their point.

Knowing, as I do from experience, what a few slaves on board a dhow really means, knowing also what the term "domestic slaves" signifies on the East Coast, I can only regret that the question of the slave-trade on the East Coast of Africa has not earlier fixed the attention of the British public, that its true character might be understood; and I cannot suppress a feeling of pride that our determined efforts at its suppression, although they have raised the ire of the petty chiefs on the coast (who, being subjects of our Indian Empire, managed to obtain the sympathy and interference of the Indian authorities, by whom, through being misinformed, the matter was misjudged), have at last had the effect of bringing the whole subject before the world.

By taking in at each port two or three slaves in a tolerably healthy condition, they can pass a considerable number off as part of the crew; and, without an interpreter who can read the ship's papers, ascertain the number allowed for the crew, number of passengers, &c., and cross-question the negroes themselves, detection is almost impossible.

When, however, the number reaches, as it often does in such vessels, to a hundred or more, it is necessary to adopt some other plan. Twenty or thirty, perhaps, are told off to represent part of the crew; the half-dozen Arabs, who are generally on board and concerned in the matter, dress up some of the women slaves, each representing one as his wife, and sometimes he is fortunate enough to have two; the remainder of the negroes, or as many as possible, are dressed up in Arab costumes, turbans, &c., and called passengers, and they too sometimes have their wives sitting by them, if the women are too plentiful to pass off in any other way. All these are usually arranged round the ship in dumb silence, which is sufficient alone to create suspicion in the experienced; and it is in this way, by taking in addition to their cargo as many negroes as they can possibly have a chance of passing through that these so-called "Legal traders" convey, perhaps, one third of the slaves to the more northern market. This plan, however, is generally frustrated, if there be on board the cruiser, a native interpreter who can detect a slave in a moment, however attired, as officers who have had any experience sometimes can, for a few questions to one or two of the poor creatures through the interpreter, —such as, where they came from, and how they got there? — are sufficient. But we, having no interpreter, were unable to put such questions, and how many vessels escaped us in consequence it is impossible to say; but we boarded on this part of the coast sometimes two or three dhows in a day, and, recollecting how full many of them were of Arabs and negroes, I feel convinced from subsequent experience that hundreds of slaves must have so run the gauntlet and passed us, through our then ignorance of this so-called "legal trader's" method of carrying slave cargoes.

It must not be lost sight of, however, that the interpreters are Arabs, who until they have associated for years with Europeans, can never understand why a successful "sharp trick," by fraud, or lie, is not a commendable achievement. It is not, therefore, to be wondered at that one of these should have been discovered—even though engaged in one of our cruisers, and receiving pay and prize-money—giving false informations to his captain in order to get the ship out of the way of a slave dhow in which he had a pecuniary interest. And while speaking of interpreters, I will add, that unless they are allowed some advantage in the shape of prize-money for captured vessels, their information will be unreliable; they make so many enemies among their own countrymen by acting as spies and informants against the slave-dealers, that they endanger their lives, even to hair-breadth escapes. If they receive pay only, there is nothing for them to gain by the taking of a slaver, and they will run no such risk, but will play into the hands of the Arabs. . . .

On the arrival of a slave dhow at Lamoo her licence ceases; if she proceeds farther towards the Arabian Coast or Persian gulf, it is at her own risk, and, acting on the old proverb that "one may as well be hung for a sheep as a lamb," the captains take in as many more slaves as they can possibly carry; and ascertaining first, by messengers sent as far north as the Juba River, the probability of the coast being pretty clear of English cruisers, they start for the northward, keeping close to the land, with the intention of running their vessels on shore if chased, with the chance of saving some of their slaves that are not drowned in the act; and also, if not molested in any way, of touching at the various ports on their way north, to obtain a handful of rice and a cup of water per slave on board, to fill up the gaps in the cargo caused by the death of many of them, and to ascertain if the coast is clear still farther to the northward. This is the illegal extension, and consequent result of a *legal slave-trade in the nineteenth century!* But it must not be supposed that the illegal part of this trade commences at the northern end of the Zanzibar dominions; on the contrary, a vast number of these dhows obtain their cargoes far south of the southern limit Quiloa, from Quillimane, Angoxa, Mozambique, Ibo, the Portuguese possessions on the coast, calling only at Quiloa to obtain the necessary pass for all of them, by possibly paying only a tax to the Custom House there for a few more to be added to their cargo at that place.

Captain Colomb also describes the difficulties of the anti-slave trade patrol, in *Slave-Catching in the Indian Ocean*, London, 1873, pp. 62-4.

WHEN the naval officer takes up the command of one of H.M.'s ships in the Indian Ocean, most probably he has no such connected idea of the northern slave trade which he is to intercept and suppress as I have given in the previous chapter. There is no 'Hand-book' to the East African slave trade, and he must acquire his knowledge of it chiefly by experience. Information respecting his powers of dealing with the slave trade in general, and instructions more or less minute, are however supplied to him in an octavo volume, the growth of many years' West Coast practice, under the title of 'Instructions for the Suppression of the Slave Trade.'

By far the greater part of this book is occupied by the text of treaties entered into between Great Britain and other European States, for the mutual allowance of search in suspected cases of slave-trading under one another's flags. Very little indeed has anything to do with the East African slave trade: very little help, guiding his proceedings, is given to the naval officer in the Indian Ocean. The book is or was, no doubt, excellent for the West Coast slave trade. But West Coast experience and East African facts are contrary the one to the other.

France and Turkey are the only civilized States upon whose flags the least suspicion of an illicit trade in slaves rests; and the suspicion does not, in the case of France, thus lie on European ships in European hands, but on Arab vessels in Arab hands. These men, it is alleged, obtain the right to fly the French flag either by a fraud on, or through the carelessness of, the Government of a French colony, and carry on their nefarious practices under its protecting folds. Consequently none of the European treaties, except such as may exist with France and Turkey, at all concern the East African slave-trade suppression.

When, however, the naval authority turns to the heading 'France,' he reads as follows: — 'There is no treaty in force between Great Britain and France for the suppression of the slave trade. None of the general instructions are therefore applicable to French vessels. Your conduct towards vessels hoisting French colours shall be regulated exclusively by the confidential instructions with which you have been furnished by the Admiralty.'

Turning now to look for 'Turkey', and 'Egypt', as under Turkey, the naval suppressor finds the name of neither State mentioned.

On the other hand, he finds the text of treaties with the following Powers given, all of whose subjects he may 'suspect to be no true men' as regards the slave trade: — Arab chiefs in the Persian Gulf; Cormoro Islands; Madagascar; Mohillah; Muscat; Persia; Zanzibar. And lastly he notices — without being, perhaps, aware that they concern him

more than all the rest put together—some special instructions
regarding the ships which own 'no name or nation.'

SLAVE RAIDERS RAIDED OFF
ZANZIBAR

The letters below were written from Zanzibar in 1865 by Captain Cornish-
Bowden of HMS *Wasp* to his wife. They were reprinted in *The Times*
of Saturday, 18 April 1964.

. . . Last night I heard a vessel was to go with slaves so I sent the
pinnace and cutter . . . The pinnace saw a dhow, fired at her, and
boarded her. The dhow with sail set ran into her and carried away
her mainmast, Lieutenant Theobold at once was thrust through his
wrist with a spear, and one poor fellow was killed. They had spears
lashed to bamboo to keep us off . . .

Lieutenant Rising in the cutter boarded aft and after much
resistance the Arabs jumped overboard and into a boat and got away
except 13 on board. They left three dead. Poor Rising appears to
have jumped into the middle very gallantly, but his left hand was
chopped nearly off at the knuckles, then he was thrust through the leg
with a spear, and in the act of falling, had a sabre cut in the
neck . . . The first we knew of it was seeing the cutter return "Union
down". In it was poor New dead. Rising unable to move covered with
blood but very cheerful . . .

I steamed out at once and brought back the dhow. On arrival I
went on board. She was crammed with slaves, as thick as bees in a
hive. No wonder my men fell about on her decks; they had to fight
standing as they could on their bodies . . . We counted 289 slaves,
mostly women and girls. Many are said to have jumped over-board
with fright . . .

14 May

I went to visit the Sultan. I spoke my mind, I think, quite as
strongly as admissible. The Sultan was willing to do anything and had
in consequence of my letter seized 250 slaves that were collected by
Northern Arabs for a cargo . . . When I told him that I did not wish
to give up the slaves or vessels, he placed the whole at my disposal;
and when I asked him to punish the Arab prisoners he said they were
mine: I could hang them or do as I pleased. That I did not want so I
convinced him that they had outraged his laws . . . He was so beastly
civil—I could not have had half a row with him . . .

As soon as they are safe to stand a little racket I shall go across to
the Seychelles with my slaves. This rainy weather puzzles me how to

stow them. I had 180 on board today, chiefly the small children and
weakly ones. As they came on board they were all put in tubs, and
well washed by the crew men with soft soap. While the tubbing was
going on I found many had small wounds . . . They are all greatly
pleased at being told they will never again be slaves.

23 May

I am very nearly to Seychelles. D.V. I shall be at anchor there
tomorrow. Thank God my wounded men are doing well . . . (Poor
Rising has had his hand amputated except the thumb and little
finger; he is terribly weak but bears up well. I have tried to cheer him
by telling him he will be promoted. I hope so if he tries, and I can
concoct a good letter.) . . .

You may fancy the state we are in. From the mizen mast aft is a
hospital, the rest of the ship a slave yard. On the whole they behave
very well, but now they have got over their awe and sea sickness
they make a great noise. We have had four die, poor creatures . . . I
cannot have them below, they smell too strong. Most of them, 19 out
of 20 are fat and jolly. Every morning they are washed in large tubs,
with the hose playing over them . . . I think they never had so much
cleaning before. Many of them are covered with craw craw, or
African itch — I think all have it more or less . . .

We have had the armourer and black-smith making a large iron to
go over and round Rising's head and chest in hopes of getting his
head upright.

The *London*, an old two-decker, was sent out to Zanzibar in 1874,
where she fulfilled the combined duties of hospital, prison, factory,
victualling yard, depot and man-of-war. She was provided with a large
number of boats, which were sent on detached service. These boats, five
of which were steam, varied in length from 42 ft to 26 ft and carried crews
from twelve to six men strong, including always a native interpreter. They
were armed with rifles, pistols and swords. The larger boats carried in
addition a 7-pounder gun. They were victualled from the ship, with often
as much as 42 days' provisions, and coaled from depots formed on little
islands on the cruising ground. Many of them were decked forward to
give protection to the crew. Otherwise they were quite open and awnings
were the only protection from sun and rain. The following is the daily
routine of one of these boats, taken from the *Anti-Slavery Reporter*, Vol.
II, Fourth Series, February 1882.

At 6 a.m. the hands are turned up, and the rain awning is furled; if
the weather is fine, a dose of quinine is then served out, after which
the boat is thoroughly scrubbed out, while the cook lights the galley
fire and prepares the breakfast. By 7 the cleaning of the boat is
generally finished, when the sun awning is spread and the men bathe,
after which breakfast is ready. This meal consists of cocoa and
biscuit. After breakfast the arms are cleaned, and when that is done

the officer, if there be one, reads prayers. Then the men are at liberty to do what they please. Smoking goes on always. Reading, sewing, and sleeping are combined with that in greater or less degree according to the individual taste. The cook prepares the dinner, which is either salt beef and "doughboys," or salt pork and pea soup, or preserved meat with flour and rice in a sort of hash. Sweet potatoes, pumpkin, and onions are added when the boat's crew are happy enough to possess any. Dinner is eaten at 12, and lime juice is served out directly afterwards. Supper is taken at 5.30, consisting of tea and biscuit. When it is dark the rain awning is spread, and at six the rum is served out. In the evening the boat's crew generally amuse themselves by singing, but at 9 all has to be quiet, and the look-out man begins his watch of which the duration depends upon the number of men in the boat. In the large boats two hours every other night is the rule, but in the small boats three hours every night. The day I have above described is an exceptionally quiet one, but usually in the course of the day two or three dhows have to be examined. When a dhow is sighted the boat gets under weigh to chase her at whatever hour it may be, unless it is convenient to go to her in the dinghy, which is a small boat for three men, about ten feet long, one of which belongs to each big boat. Suppose a dhow to be sighted making in for the land at a distance from the boat too great to allow of the dinghy being sent to board her, the awnings are at once furled, the anchor weighed, and sail made. On approaching the chase a rifle is fired across her bows to make her lower her sail. Supposing the people in the dhow do not hear, or do not choose to take any notice of this first shot, it is repeated until they do, each time pitching the bullet a little closer. The dhow's not stopping need not be proof of her being a slaver, for a trading dhow does not like a delay of an hour, and if she sees a chance of getting off without being searched she will attempt it. Suppose, however, that on this occasion the dhow cannot escape and lowers her sail, the boat on coming up to her heaves to, and the officer or coxswain goes to the dhow in the dinghy with the interpreter and another man. If she is full of slaves, which is seldom the case, there is no doubt about what should be done: but if she is full of cargo and passengers, then comes trouble. Every person who can be suspected of being a slave must be taken apart and cross-examined in order to prevent his being smuggled across in the way I have above described—for in the presence of the owner or agent a slave would be too much frightened to confess his condition. After the examination of all suspicious-looking persons on board, the cargo has to be searched; that, however, can be very quickly done, as the officer can readily judge whether any one is likely to be concealed in it. I

think that slaves are not often smuggled across in cargo. The dhow is
finally allowed to depart when the officer is satisfied of the honesty of
her proceedings, or is convinced that she is, as the blockaders express
it, "no good".

Captain Colomb, in *Slave Catching in the Indian Ocean*, p. 229,
describes the life of an officer on one of these boats.

Incessant boardings of dhows; constant and prolonged examinations
generally resulting in acquittal. Perpetual rushing to sea at all hours
of day and night; an eternal weighing and anchoring. Changing a
dry boat's crew for a wet and exhausted one; substituting a fresh boat
for one damaged under a rolling dhow. Noting a wind every day
increasing, and a coal supply every day decreasing.

W. Cope Devereux, in *The Cruise of the Gorgon*, London, 1869, pp.
109-11, further describes the slave dhows.

THE TRADE BY SEA.

The southern dhows are employed carrying slaves or merchandize,
whichever turns up first, their crews generally consisting of Arabs and
natives mixed. The northern dhows leave the Persian Gulf about the
end of March, with the last of the north-east monsoon, laden with
putrid shark, &c., for Zanzibar.

Here they dispose of their offensive cargo as slave food, and then
with the south-west monsoon begin their work. Commencing at
Zanzibar, kidnapping, and running off with all the men, women,
and children they can lay their hands upon, and carrying on this
detestable inhuman pillage as far as the Juba Islands, when, having
taken in the last supply of water, they make for the ports of Soor and
Muscat, in the Persian Gulf, their head slave markets.

The crews of these vessels are the most cruel and degraded race
that can be imagined. They are called Soree pirates . . .

HORRORS OF THE TRADE.

It is difficult to imagine the real horrors of this dhow traffic,
especially with the northerners. They have a voyage of nearly 1500
miles, from Zanzibar to the Persian Gulf, and during the whole time
the slaves are exposed to the weather quite naked, and are very badly
fed, their daily rations being just sufficient to keep life and soul
together, and sometimes not even that. From daylight until evening
the wretched slaves sit under the rays of a tropical sun, half famished.
About sunset a meal is served out to them. From a mess of burnt
boiled millet seed, a platterfull is given to a crowd of thirty, who flock

round it, sitting upon their haunches; old and young, big and little, some of the women having babies slung behind them; they all dip into it with their hands, rolling it into balls, and feeding themselves as turkeys are crammed. After each has had about three small balls, the dish is finished and the last mouthful is scrambled and fought for. The grains left are then picked up from the dirty planks, and as might is right, the strong have the lion's share, and the weak go to the wall. After this a drink of water is allowed, then they are left to hunger and thirst, cold and heat, cramp and stench, for the next twenty-four hours, and very often for two days, and this is considered good feeding. Add to this the smell of these dhows — a conglomeration of the vilest odours ever mingled; the poor slaves having hardly any convenience of any kind.

I was once on board a captured dhow, with a cargo of slaves, for a whole day, and the result of the stench was fever and sickness, of which I have a vivid recollection.

A party of our men were prostrated by it. Articles of furniture, &c., taken from these vessels never lose their horrid smell, however much they may be cleansed or purified.

Generally speaking, about one-half the cargo reaches its destination alive, the mortality being caused by starvation and disease, and this when the dhow is sailing along quietly enough, with no cruisers in sight. But, on the other hand, when chased, what frightfully cruel deeds are perpetrated by the heartless Arabs! The poor slaves are very often murdered and thrown overboard. Near Zanzibar a case of this kind occurred. A dhow had slaves on board, and hearing that a cruiser's boats were on her track, the Arabs commenced a wholesale butchery of the slaves, cutting their throats and tossing them into the sea.

The English boats got to them in time to save about fifty or sixty, at least twenty or thirty having been despatched.

Following the anti-slave trade treaty of 1873, and increased vigilance of the anti-slave trade patrol at sea, there was much smuggling of slaves from the mainland across to Zanzibar and Pemba. The following is an account of how this was done, at the year 1882, taken from the *Anti-Slavery Reporter*, Vol. II, Fourth Series. February 1882.

The dhow is prepared for the reception of the slaves by having sand or sticks laid down in her hold. No extra provision or water is considered necessary. The slaves are shipped at night, accompanied either by their owners in person or by their agents. These people are generally well armed, but for them to make any use of their weapons against our boats is the rarest occurrence. After the slaves are on

board, the dhow leaves as soon as possible. If the land to which they
are bound is sighted by day they generally lower their sail and wait till
it is dark, when they again hoist their sail and run in till quite close to
the land, when, as a rule, they again lower their sail, which makes
them nearly invisible. They then quietly paddle in to the shore, run
the dhow's bow on the beach, and land the slaves with the dealers
who have come in charge of the cargo. If they have landed on the
main island of Zanzibar or Pemba their trouble is nearly over, for our
men have not the right to search for slaves in these places. The slaves
can be taken at once to their destination, or, if the Sultan's soldiers
are in the neighbourhood, they can be hidden in the bush and taken
to their journey's end as opportunity offers. But if they have landed
on one of the above-described off-lying islands they are still in danger
from our boats, as the crews are allowed to search these islands and
seize any newly landed slaves that they find. In this case the crew
clean the inside of the dhow thoroughly, so that no trace of her last
employment may be left. They very often cut wood in order to gain
the appearance of a trading dhow. The next morning the dhow sails
into her port, and is very likely examined on the way by the man-of-
war's boat whose watch she had the previous night evaded. The safe
arrival of the cargo is then made known to the consignee, who
charters canoes, which the next night go to the islands and bring over
the slaves who have been all day hidden in the bush.

It was not an unusual tactic of the slavers to run their dhows ashore to
escape capture by the British naval anti-slave trade patrol. The following
are two instances of this, the first from the report of HM Commissioners to
Earl Russell, dated 19 September 1862.

A dhow of from 150 to 175 tons was captured sixteen miles north of
Brava, April 4, 1862. On the same day at daylight, a dhow was
observed to the north of Brava, rounding to the northward. At 9 a.m.
the *Ariel* stood for her, when she immediately bore up for the land,
upon which the *Ariel* made chase. At 11 a.m. the dhow anchored on
the edge of the surf, about 16 miles north of Brava, and the *Ariel* at
12.20 anchored about 800 yards off her. It was observed that she was
full of slaves, and that the crew with their effects were escaping to the
land. Captain Oldfield proceeded with two gigs of the *Ariel* and
boarded the dhow, which was thoroughly equipped for the Slave
Trade, and had from 80 to 100 slaves on board. When boarded the
crew had to cut her cables, she was fast drifting into the surf. Her
position rendered it impossible to remove the slaves, one man
excepted. The dhow drifted on to the beach, and the boats were in
the most imminent peril: that commanded by Captain Oldfield being

swamped, and the crew with difficulty saved, while the shore was lined with armed men, who with muskets and spears attacked the boats and such of the slaves as attempted to make for them. Captain Oldfield, thereupon declared the dhow seized as a slaver, and she soon afterwards became a total wreck. The slaves escaped to the shore, where they were seized by the armed men, apparently Somali Arabs, and the dhow being deserted, her destruction was completed by shelling her. She appeared to be from 150 to 175 tons burthen.

SP. Vol. LXXI, 1863, No. 25. Case No. 15.

The second is taken from the *Anti-Slavery Reporter* Vol. 15. No. 9., 16 September 1867.

The second day after leaving Zanzibar we took a dhow with 150 slaves, almost all children, or boys under 14: and as they had only started they were in good health, all but a few who are significantly called the lanterns by the sailors, because, I suppose, you can almost see through them. As we caught the small-pox, we made our way to Aden at once, calling at one or two places on the way, and landed them all except three who died on the way. We are now at anchor under Guardafui, which all dhows bound for Mahilla, must pass, and we hope to pick up several more.

Oct 6th — Tomorrow we start for Aden, having had a most successful cruise — taken seven dhows, and have now on board 393 liberated slaves, making 550 since we left Zanzibar. It is rather exciting work. As a sample I will tell you what happened the other morning, which was the best fun we had. We just turned round Guardafui at dawn, with a dhow in tow, when we sighted another; so anchoring our one, away we were after the other, who hauled close in to shore, which, luckily for us, is very high, and when we got near, he ran ashore under a steep cliff 1300 feet high, and bundled all his slaves out on the beach. But as we were close, we sent a few 8-inch shot over him, which frightened them all, and I went ashore with two boats' crews and chased them, and surrounded all the slaves, to the number of 117, and got them off, the Arabs being in too great fright to do anything but run. I do not think they kept more than three out of the cargo. The Somalis here act the part of jackals; as soon as they see a dhow coming, or hear our guns, they rush down, and as soon as we allow them to approach, which we do after we have got all we want, in they rush, and in five minutes nothing worth a farthing is left of the dhow.

The following descriptions of encounters with slave-dhows are also taken from the *Anti-Slavery Reporter*, the first from Vol. II, Fourth

Series, January 1882, and the second from Vol. VIII, Fourth Series, November-December 1888.

THE ENCOUNTER WITH A SLAVE-DHOW.

Later Particulars.

As we go to Press, full details of this cowardly act have arrived. They present a terrible picture of a gallant struggle on behalf of the oppressed, in which a brave officer was overborne in his almost single-handed encounter with a gang of pirates — some of the worst ruffians on the face of the earth. From the official report transmitted to the Admiralty by Acting-Commander Goodridge we extract the following: —

"From personal knowledge I know that Captain Brownrigg never boarded French dhows, but was in the habit of going alongside to verify their papers. On this occasion he appears to have had the same purpose, as he told the boat's crew to be careful not to board without direct orders, apparently intending a mere cursory examination, and no detention whatever, as he did not arm the boat's crew, and directed the time alongside to be noted.

"He went alongside without hailing or stopping her in any way, the wind being light, and the dhow scarcely forging ahead.

    *   *   *   *   *   *

"As the coxwain was standing on the stem of the boat, in the act of making fast with the hook rope, he caught sight of some eight or ten men crouched in the bottom of the boat with guns at the "ready" position. He sang out to the captain aft, when they rose up and fired; he flung the hook at them, and closed with one, both falling overboard together.

"The Arabs, the number of whom is variously estimated at from fifteen to twenty-five, then jumped into the pinnace with drawn swords and clubbed guns. As their first fire seems to have killed one man (a stoker) outright, mortally wounded another, and severely wounded two others of the boat's crew, the Arabs found but little difficulty in driving the rest, unarmed as they were, overboard.

"Captain Brownrigg and his steward were the only two left, and both were in the after part of the boat. He appears to have seized a rifle at the first volley, and fired, knocking an Arab over; but before he could reload, three or four of them rushed aft to attack him, getting on the top of the canopy and at the sides, but he, clubbing his rifle, kept them at bay, fighting with a determination that has filled the survivors, who were then in the water, unable to get on board, with the greatest admiration, they describing him as fighting like a lion.

"He knocked two of his assailants over, but was unable to get at them properly, owing to the structure of the boat (as I have before described), he being in the stern sheets, whilst they were above him on the canopy, cutting at him with their long swords, but fearing to jump down and close with him. As he knocked one over, another took his place.

"The first wound that seems to have hampered him in the gallant fight was a cut across the forehead, from which the blood, pouring over his face, partially blinded him. He was then cut across the hands, the fingers being severed from the left and partially so from the right one; and, badly wounded in both elbows, he could no longer hold the rifle.

"He then appears to have tried to get hold of any of his foes, or of anything wherewith to fight on, but, blinded as he was, his efforts were in vain. He fought thus for upwards of twenty minutes, keeping his face to his assailants, and having no thought, or making no effort, to seek safety by jumping overboard. At length he was shot through the heart and fell dead, having, besides the fatal one, received no less than twenty wounds, most of them of a severe, and two of a mortal nature."

The Sultan of Zanzibar, in a subsequent letter written to a friend in this country, explains the steps that he had taken in concert with the French Consul, to capture the dhow and her villainous crew. We believe that a telegram of a still later date has reached England, stating that not only has the dhow been captured, but that her captain had died from the wounds inflicted upon him in self-defence by the brave but unfortunate Captain Brownrigg. The whole question of the protection given by the French flag to Slave-dhows in East Africa will have to be taken up by the respective Governments.

COMMANDER GISSING TO REAR-ADMIRAL FREMANTLE.

"OSPREY," AT ADEN, *September*, 18, 1888.

SIR, — I have the honour to report that, in consequence of information obtained by me, and reported in my letter of proceedings, I left Perim on the night of the 4th September, and proceeded to cruise between Mokha Point and Ras Muteinah, on the morning of Sunday, the 16th, at daylight, being about seven miles from Mokha Point. I sighted three dhows standing to the northward, the wind being south-westerly. I took up a position about half-a-mile to leeward of them, and between them and the shore, when I fired several blank charges to bring them to. They immediately altered course in various directions, making for the shore. I then fired several shots across their bows, also hailing them to lower their sails. They paid no attention, but still endeavoured to get away. I then, feeling sure they must be Slavers, went to quarters, firing from the 7-pounder and 64-pounders at their masts. Several shots went through their sails, but none striking the masts or halyards, I saw that it was necessary to use the machine-guns, and ordered the Gardners in the top to open fire, a shot from one of which killed the captain of the largest dhow, when she came into the wind and lowered her sail. I then lowered a boat fully armed, and sent Mr. JOHN W. H. BUDGE, gunner, in her, to take charge of the capture. The second dhow shortly after lowered her sail, but the third had gone some distance away. I gave chase to her, repeatedly sending shots through her sails, but they still continued their course, but the fire from the Gardners caused them also to give in, when I lowered a boat armed, Mr. JAMES KEAST, boatswain, in charge, and took the dhow in tow to rejoin the other two, now some three miles away. While I was doing this the second dhow rehoisted her sails and attempted to get away, but Mr. JOHN W. H. BUDGE, gunner, being in the first dhow, some 500 yards away, opened fire on her with his rifles, and they then lowered their sail and gave in. I then took all the crews, agents, and owners of the Slaves on board, making them prisoners, thirty-three in number, consisting of Arabs from Turkish ports of Red Sea, and Dankali merchants. I then removed all the Slaves on board the *Osprey*, 204 in number, took the three dhows in tow, and proceeded to Aden. Before proceeding I caused to be buried the captain of dhow who was killed; also, I regret to say, four Slaves who were killed in the dhows. This I feel to be a great blot on the proceedings; but still I feel assured that unless I had made use of the Gardner guns no capture would have been made. The big guns were never fired at the dhows, but only at their masts, and the crews, when brought on board, stated that they did not mind the big guns, but it was the bullets from the guns up the masts which made them lower their sails.

The procedure of adjudication at a Prize Court in cases of captured slave dhows was simple and informal. The chief evidence was the personal presence of captured slaves, as described by Captain Colomb's *Slave Catching in the Indian Ocean,* pp. 262-3.

The Resident (the civil governor) is ex-officio the judge of the Court, and practically he is the whole Court, vice-Admiral, Judge, and Registrar. The Court is held generally in one of the rooms of the Residency, or other convenient place. The form is very simple. The Court is prayed to exercise its jurisdiction; and the Captain of the capturing vessel, or other officer deputed by him, together with the necessary witnesses, attend on a given day with certificates of the number of slaves taken out of the vessels, the measurements of the latter, and a certificate of their destination. The witnesses — one or two, then state, on oath, the circumstances of the capture; and if the case is clear, a decree of condemnation of the vessel as lawful prize to the capturing ship, follows immediately. . . . In the six cases of capture, or destruction, which we offered for adjudication, it was necessary only to take formal evidence, the whole thing was over in an hour and a half, and we returned to ship, happy, in the possession of documents equivalent to a demand on the English Treasury for about £2200.

See also SP LXXI 1875, No. 66, Captain Prideaux: 28-7-1874.

In the same book, Colomb on p. 217 shows the Pro-forma of a Pass issued by the Sultan of Zanzibar to his subjects so that their dhows would be free from interference by the British Anti-Slave Trade patrol.

Know by these presents all our benevolent and most respectable friends who are resident on men-of-war, and travelling from east to west and from west to east continually, (may God give a helping hand to you!) that this is the vessel — — belonging to — — coming from — — going to — —. Besides the captain and owner, there are on board — — seamen and passengers. 'Do not throw any obstacle in their way, but fulfil all the obligations of friendship, and all the respects of familiarity'.

In the Court of HBM's Agent and Consul Gl., Zanzibar, Admiralty Jurisdiction Cause No. 39 of 1888. Decree:

Our Sovereign Lady the Queen against a native vessel name unknown, sailing under no colours and having no papers whereof both the owner and the master are unknown, her tackle, apparel and furniture, and also against eight male and twenty-one female slaves seized as liable to forefeiture by J.E. Blaxland Esquire, a Commander in the Royal Navy in Command of H.M.S. *Griffin*. Before Ernest Berkeley Esquire, Her Majesty's Vice Consul and Acting Judge at Zanzibar on the 13th day of August 1888.

Appeared personally Charles E. Hutchins holding the rank of Gunner in Her Majesty's ship *Griffin* and produced his sworn declaration setting out the circumstances under which the native vessel name unknown, sailing under no colours and having no papers, whereof both the owner and master are unknown, of the description and dimension specified in the annexed Certificate of admeasurement taken by the Captors, was seized by him together with eight male and twenty-one female slaves off Pemba on the 9th day of August 1888. In the said Judge having examined the evidence produced by the captors and default of any person appearing for the defence having sufficient proof that the said vessel at the time of her capture was engaged in conveying a cargo of slaves, which the said twenty-nine slaves formed part of, in contravention of Treaties existing between Great Britain and Zanzibar, do adjudge the said vessel, her tackle, apparel and furniture together with the said slaves to have been lawfully seized and to be forfeited to our Sovereign Lady the Queen and do condemn the same accordingly, and I further declare that the sinking of the vessel on the spot was inevitable under the circumstances set forth in the Captor's Certificate of Destruction.

In testimony whereof I have signed the present Decree and have caused my seal of office to be affixed thereto this 13th day of August 1888.

Signed Ernest Berkely,
H.M. Vice Consul & Acting Judge.

Inclosure with above: *Certificate as to Destruction of Prize*

I, the undersigned, Mr. Charles E. Hutchins, holding the Rank of Gunner in Her Britannica Majesty's Navy, and belonging to Her Majesty's Ship *Griffin*, do hereby certify that, on the Ninth day of August 1888, I directed a survey to be held on the Dhow, or Native Vessel, called the Name 'Unknown' detained by me on the Ninth day of August 1888, on the ground that she engaged in the Slave Trade, and that the result of such Survey was that the said Dhow leaked so badly, that she soon sank in deep water, and the said dhow has therefore been destroyed by my orders.

Given under my hand this Ninth day of August 1888.
Chas E. Hutchins, Gunner.
Approved by me this 13th day of August.
J.E. Blaxland, Commander,
Commanding H.M.S. *Griffin*

There was unfortunately no treaty between Great Britain and France to enable British ships of war to search dhows flying French colours with a view to their detention if they were found to be engaged in the slave trade. Thus the utmost British naval officers might do was to board them in order to examine their papers. If these were found to be correct, their proceedings could be no further interfered with, and no question could be put to anyone on board. Thus permission readily given by the French to the Arabs to use their colours decidedly increased the difficulties attendant on the suppression of the slave trade. This abuse of the use of the French flag neutralized British endeavours to end the slave trade on the high seas.

British Admiralty instructions to commanders of squadrons in 1859 urged extreme caution, as shown in E. Hertslet, *Treaties*, vii, London 1891, pp. 345-6.

"You are not to capture, visit, or in any way interfere with vessels of France; and you will give strict instructions to the commanding officers of cruisers under your orders to abstain therefrom. At the same time you will remember that the King of the French is far from claiming that the flag of France should give immunity to those who have no right to bear it; and that Great Britain will not allow vessels of other nations to escape visit and examination by merely hoisting a French flag, or the flag of any other nation with which Great Britain has not, by existing Treaty, the right of search. Accordingly, when from intelligence which the officer commanding Her Majesty's cruisers may have received, or from the manoeuvres of the vessel, or other sufficient cause, he may have reason to believe that the vessel does not belong to the nation indicated by her colours, he is, if the state of the weather will admit of it, to go ahead of the suspected vessel, after communicating his intention by hailing, and to drop a boat on board of her to ascertain her nationality . . .; and if she prove really to be a vessel of the nation designated by her colours, and one which he is not authorized to search, he is to lose no time in quitting her; offering to note on the papers of the vessel the cause of his having suspected her nationality, as well as the number of minutes the vessel was detained . . .

"Of course in cases when suspicion of the commander turns out to be well founded, and the vessel boarded proves, notwithstanding her colours, not to belong to the nation designated by these colours, the commander of Her Majesty's cruisers will deal with her as he would have been authorized and required to do had she not hoisted a false flag . . .

"To inquire into the nature of the cargo, or the commercial operations of the vessel, or any other fact, in short, than that of nationality of the vessel, is prohibited; every other search and inspection whatever is absolutely forbidden."

As a result of the French ruling, Arab dhow owners fulfilled the domicile claims by acquiring patches of land in French colonies, at Obok, Madagascar and the Comoro Islands: they were then granted the necessary papers to fly the French flag. SP LXVI 1864, Incl. 8 No. 82, M. Jablonski to Lt. Col. Playfair, 15-9-1863, gives an extract from 'Acte de Francisation' of a boat belonging to Selemani bin Djouma domiciled at Ambanourow.

In the name of the Emperor of the French, the Commandant of Nossi-Bé declares that the Sieur Selemani bin Djouma 'Francais domicilié' at Ambanourow is entitled to be the proprieter of the boat 'Ambanourow' below described, which has been registered at the port of Hellville (Nossi-Bé). *Seen* the Acts establishing the measurement of the boat, the said boat is French property, and that the oath has been received.

Seen also the recognisance and the security bond deposited in the Post Office, Nossi Bé, on the 27th November, relating to the registry of "Francisation", exceptionally granted in the Colony. The present Act is given by us in order to confer the privilige of navigating under the French flag.

In consequence we pray and require all Sovereigns etc.

And Horace Waller of the Universities Mission to Central Africa, stated, in evidence before the Select Committee of 1870/71 on the East African Slave Trade, that

I have seen a French ship lying at the island of Johanna, crammed with slaves, with one of our men-of-war within cable's length of her, and the poor creatures jumping overboard and swimming to us, to protect them, and the Arabs would say to us, 'there is a Frenchman there full of slaves, if it was one of our ships you would burn her directly, why do you not go and take her?

A despatch from the Admiralty to the Foreign Office reported that Commander Baker who boarded a suspected slave dhow

found the dhow's papers to be correct but 'All the time the officers were on board the Arabs continued to make as much noise as possible by shouting and stamping their feet, but notwithstanding this the presence of living creatures could be distinctly heard from below the hatches; that, combined with the stench, convinced me that she was also full of slaves, which fact was also communicated by the master of Case No. 2 to the officer on his boarding that dhow. Nevertheless under the circumstances and the very delicate nature of the instructions I reluctantly allowed her to proceed'.

FOCP 6913/140, 17 November 1896.

And we have another detailed description of the boarding of a dhow flying French colours, and the indisputable evidence of slaving to which the use of the French flag by the Arabs conduced, in a statement in regard to the French dhow *Fatheklee*, detained on Sunday, 9 April 1893.

On boarding the dhow 'Fatheklee' under French colours, at about 11.40 a.m. on 9th April in English Passage, she then being about 2 miles from the anchorage etc. I was met by the captain, who presented French papers dated 7th April; they were apparently correct, showing a list of 57 passengers and a crew of thirty. Whilst examining the papers, one of my boats crew lifted the hatch and at once a number of children (17) made a rush on deck, they having been stowed under close hatches amongst the wood cargo; as passengers going of their own free will would certainly not be stowed away in such a manner, and as the passenger list, where ages were mentioned, showed ages from 16 to 40, and these were all children, I considered myself justified in ordering the captain of the dhow to lower his sail, and in instituting a further search, in the forepart of the dhow we found five more stowed in crevices of the wood cargo, and finding the cabin under the poop locked I demanded the key, which after some demur was produced; on entering we found two women and five boys in total darkness, and with no ventilation, the stern and side windows having sheets of tin nailed over them, and matting again over that; we sent them on deck, and a light being struck, I saw a small trap hatch in the deck which I at once ordered to be opened; as the hatch was lifted a most piteous cry came up from the utter darkness below, and twenty little arms were stretched up to us out of this horrible hole; we lifted one or two at a time, five or six women, and upwards of forty children: the heat and stench were something fearful, the place being without vestige of ventilation, swarming with rats, cockroaches, and other vermin, and a close hatch over it. When the children were freed they cried most piteously for water, which was of course at once given them; they then asked eagerly for food, and I saw one of them devouring orange peel.

When the dhow took in to anchorage, the scene was piteous, 'the women and children struggling for the food; in fact we had considerable difficulty at first in preventing the smaller and weaker ones, the children of apparently 6 or 7 years of age, being injured in the rush. The captain stated that they were all on board and going to Muscat of their own free will, and they had all been before the French Consul. I then had them interrogated, individually, and they all denied that they had ever been taken before the French Consul at all, and seventy of them declared that they had been brought on board at night against their own will during the last three nights and kept under close hatches ever since whilst seven stated that they were willing to go to Muscat, there being seventy-seven in all, which with thirty-seven passengers and crew made a total of 114 persons on board. The dhow was fully provisioned and well armed.

I can fully substantiate these statements by the evidence of Mr. Jennings (Gunner) who accompanied me, and that of the boat's crew under my command.'

A. B. GRENFELL, Senior Lieutenant. April 11, 1893.

FOCP 6454/180

The concern felt by British officials at Zanzibar over the use of the French flag by Arab slavers is expressed in the following taken from C. E. B. Russell's *General Rigby, Zanzibar and the Slave Trade*, London, 1935, p. 145. Rigby, the British Consul, arriving at Zanzibar in 1858,

found a most active slave trade carried on at Zanzibar itself, and along the coast by French vessels . . . French vessels went escorted by French men-of-war, and slaves were taken to Reunion and Mayotta . . . There is a French ship here now full of slaves, they all wear a wooden ticket round the neck . . . they pretend that it is not a slave trade, that the negroes are only engaged to serve for a term of years and go willing . . . On reaching the deck of the French ship the ceremony of engaging the slaves as 'free labourers' is gone through by an Arab interpeter, who asks them in the presence of the delegate (a French official) whether they voluntarily engage to serve for five years at Reunion. The interpreter assures the delegate that the slave is willing to become a 'free labourer' at Reunion in every instance. The delegate cannot speak the native language and does not know what question the slave is asked, nor the nature of his reply, but being assured by the Arab that the slave is willing to go to Reunion, the French delegate is satisfied.

And Rennel Rodd, British consul at Zanzibar, to Lord Rosebery, blamed the widespread kidnapping and smuggling of slaves from Zanzibar on the Suri Arabs, who, sailing under the French flag, came down to the island with the northeast monsoon, lodged in the Malindi quarter of Zanzibar town for a few months, and from there carried on their activities.

These Suri Arabs who come down at certain seasons are an unmitigated curse to this island, at their instigation the whole underground machinery of slave-dealing and barter is given a new encouragement . . . I do not wish to be understood to imply that the French flag is issued without any apparent reason, simply on payment of fees, but the Arabs seem thoroughly to understand that it is easy to procure it if they are willing to face an expense which the lucrative business of slave-running with impunity well repays. There are various ways in which the French flag can be secured, but the simplest and surest is the purchase of a hut or a few square metres of land in Nossi Bé or some other French island. It is thus not too much to state that French protection can actually be purchased for a few rupees, and it would be strange if the slave traders and all whose hands are against the Local Governments did not avail themselves of this resource, as we find to our cost that they do . . . It is by such means as these, if not on even less warrantable grounds, that scoundrels from the Persian Gulf and the Gulf of Oman, from regions which have as little connection with France as the planet Jupiter, are enabled to carry havoc into this Protectorate and to foster a trade which all the rest of civilization is loyally co-operating to suppress.

FOCP 6454/180, 14 April 1893

VI
ANTI-SLAVERY AND ANTI-SLAVE TRADE DECREES AND TREATIES: THEIR AFTERMATH

The issuing of anti-slave trade and anti-slavery decrees and treaties continued throughout the nineteenth century. The main decrees are set out here, and the majority are taken from C. U. Aitchison, *A Collection of Treaties, Engagements and Sanads relating to India and Neighbouring Countries,* Delhi, 1933. Britain's first attempt to check the northern Arab slave trade took the form of treaties with the Arab rulers in the Persian Gulf area. On 8 January 1820, Britain concluded with the principal sheikhs of the Pirate Coast and the Sheikh of Bahrein a General Treaty of Peace, containing a clause declaring the transport of slaves as piracy, and forbidden to the signatory powers.

The carrying off of slaves, men, women, or children from the coast of Africa or elsewhere, and the transporting them in vessels, is plunder and piracy, and the friendly Arabs shall do nothing of this nature.

Aitchison, Vol. XI. p. 245.

But the main culprits in the East African slave trade were the Omani Arabs; and it was with Sayyid Said, Sultan of Oman 1804-56 who also claimed dominion over Zanzibar and the East African coast, that the British made the Moresby Treaty of 1822. As will be seen by the terms of this treaty, it aimed at the suppression of the foreign slave trade with Christian nations, but not with Mohammedan countries, nor within the Sultan of Oman's dominions in Asia and Africa. Permission was given under the treaty to British cruisers to seize slave ships east of a line as defined in the treaty; this permission was not extended to the Indian Navy until 1839 when the 1822 treaty was re-confirmed.

TREATY CONCLUDED WITH THE IMAM OF MUSCAT FOR THE SUPPRESSION OF SLAVERY, – 1822.

TRANSLATION.

In the name of the Most High God!

Particulars of the requisitions which were made by Captain Moresby, Commander of the Ship *Meani*, who arrived at the port of Muscat on the 9th of the sacred (month of) Zilhujjah 1237 (27th August 1822) from the Island of Mauritius, on the part of the Governor Sir Robert Farquhar, Bahadur.

In the name of the Most High God!

Answers to the requisitions which were made by Captain Moresby on the part of the Governor Sir Robert Farquhar, Bahadur, may his glory be eternal! which (requisitions) are mentioned on the back of this paper.

ARTICLE 1.

That you (the Imam) instruct all the Officers in your dominions to prevent the subjects from selling slaves to Christians of all nations.

ARTICLE 1.

That we did write last season to all our Officers to prohibit the sale of slaves to all the Christian nations, and we will send further instructions to them on the subject.

ARTICLE 2.

That you do issue orders to all your Officers, who are on your part throughout your dominions, as well in Zanzibar as in other places, to the the effect that if they discover persons on board any Arab vessel buying slaves for the purpose of taking them to Christian countries, they (the Officers) should seize such vessel with all that she may contain, and should send to you the Nakhoda (*i.e.*, the Commander) and the crew, in order that you may punish them.

ARTICLE 2.

That we will send orders to all our Officers who are employed throughout our dominions to the effect that if they find any Arab vessel buying slaves for the purpose of taking them to Christian countries, they must seize the vessel and inflict punishment on persons connected with her, even if they be bound for the Island of Madagascar.

ARTICLE 3.

That it shall be obligatory on the crew of every vessel that shall clandestinely convey slaves to Christian countries to give, on their return to an Arab port, information to the Governor of that port, in order that he may punish the Commander, and that if they fail to give the information, all shall suffer punishment.

ARTICLE 3.

That we will instruct our Officers and notify throughout our dominions that the crew of a vessel conveying slaves for sale to Christian countries are required, on their return to an Arab port, to give information to the Governor of the port in order that he may punish the Commander, but that if they conceal (the fact), all shall suffer punishment.

ARTICLE 4.

That Your Highness give us a written order, on your part to the Governor of Zanzibar and your other Governors in that quarter, to the

ARTICLE 4.

That a written order which you wish to have, permitting the stationing of a person on your part in Zanzibar and the neighbouring effect that they do allow a person to be stationed on our part in any place in those countries which we shall see fit, and that they do allow us a place for residence in order that we may obtain intelligence of any vessel that may convey slaves to Christian countries.

parts for the purpose of obtaining intelligence of the sale of slaves to Christian nations, has been granted, and will reach through the hands of the respected Captain Moresby. May his dignity endure for ever!

ARTICLE 5.

That you give us a written permission that if we find any vessel laden with slaves for sale, carrying them to Christian countries, after four months from the date of such written permission, we may seize her.

ARTICLE 5.

That written permission which you wish to have, permitting you, after four months, to seize vessels conveying slaves for sale to Christian countries, will reach through the hands of the said Captain.

ARTICLE 6.

That you do write to all your Governors that on the sailing of every vessel they shall write out a pass for her, stating clearly what port she is leaving and what she is bound to, in order that if our ships should meet a vessel having no pass, but having on board slaves for sale and proceeding in the direction of the Christian countries, they (the British ships) may seize her; such a vessel, if found within the line of the Island of Madagascar and the neighbourhood of Zanzibar and Lamoo, to be carried into Muscat for punishment by you; but if found sailing beyond the Island of Madagascar and in the sea of Mauritius, to be seized by themselves (British vessels), and this (to take place) after four months from the date of the written permission.

ARTICLE 6.

That we will write to our Governors regarding the granting of a pass to every vessel proceeding on a voyage, specifying therein the port she sails from, and the port she is bound to, and you may seize every vessel you may fall in with beyond the Island of Madagascar and in the sea of Mauritius after four months from the date of the written permission alluded to in the fifth requisition; and if any vessel be found on this side, the matter should come to us, provided she do not possess a pass from the Governor of the port of departure.

Here end the answers to the six requisitions, and they have been written by the most humble Abdul Kahir bin Syud Mahomed Ali Majid by order of his master, who commands his obedience, Syud Saeed bin Syud Sultan bin Imam Ahmed bin Saeed Al Boo Saeedee.

Written on the 17th of the sacred (month of) Zilhujjah 1237, one thousand two hundred and thirty-seven of the Hegira (4th September 1822).

This is signed by the humble Saeed bin Sultan with his own hand.
SEAL OF SAEED BIN SULTAN BIN AHMED.

TRANSLATION.

In the name of the Most High God!

Particulars of an additional requisition made by CAPTAIN MORESBY for the suppression (of the sale of) slaves carried on board vessels to Christian countries.

It is necessary to define the line beyond which we may seize Arab carrying slaves to Christian countries after four months from the date of the written permission mentioned in the fifth requisition. Let it be understood that all vessels on board of which there may be slaves for sale, and which may be found by our ships beyond a straight line drawn from the Cape Delkada and passing six zains (*i.e.*, sixty miles) from Socotra on to Dieu, shall be seized by our ships, but that vessels found beyond the said line driven by stress of weather or by any other unavoidable circumstance shall not be seized.

In the name of the Most High God!

Answer to the additional requisition made by CAPTAIN MORESBY for the suppression (of the sale of) slaves carried to Christian countries.

I permit the Captains of ships belonging to the English Government to seize all Arab vessels carrying slaves to Christian countries which may be found beyond a straight line drawn from the Cape Delkada and passing sixty miles from Socotra on to Dieu* after the date of the written permission mentioned in the fifth requisition, but not to seize vessels found beyond the line which may have been driven by stress of weather or any other unavoidable circumstance.

Written by Abdul Kahir bin Syud Mahomed bin Syud Majid by order of his master, who commands his obedience, Saeed bin

*Here is omitted four months.

Syud Sultan Imam Ahmed bin
Saeed Al Boo Saeedee.
*Written on the 22nd Zilhujjah
1237, 9th September 1822.*

Aitchison, Vol. XI, pp. 289–91.

In December 1839 Sultan Said agreed with the British Resident in the
Persian Gulf to add three additional articles to the treaty of 1822,
authorizing the right of search and extending the boundary laid down in
the treaty of 1822 from Diu Head to Pasni, the eastern boundary of Said's
possession on the Baluchistan coast.

TRANSLATION of ADDITIONAL ARTICLES regarding the SUPPRESSION of
the FOREIGN SLAVE TRADE entered into by HIS HIGHNESS SAEED SYUD
BIN SULTAN: the IMAM of MUSCAT, — 1839.

I agree that the following Articles be added to the above Treaty
concluded by Captain Moresby on the aforesaid date: —

ARTICLE 1.

That the Government cruizers, whenever they may meet any vessel
belonging to my subjects beyond a direct line drawn from Cape
Delgado passing two degrees seaward of the Island of Socotra and
ending at Pussein, and shall suspect that such vessel is engaged in the
slave trade, the said cruizers are permitted to detain and search it.

ARTICLE 2.

Should it on examination be found that any vessel belonging to my
subjects is carrying slaves, whether men, women, or children, for sale
beyond the aforesaid line, then the government cruizers shall seize
and confiscate such vessel and her cargo. But if the said vessel shall
pass beyond the aforesaid line owing to stress of weather, or other
case of necessity not under control, then she shall not be seized.

ARTICLE 3

As the selling of males and females, whether grown up or young,
who are "Hoor" or free, is contrary to the Mahomedan religion, and
whereas the Soomalees are included in the Hoor or free, I do hereby
agree that the sale of males and females, whether young or old of the
Soomalee tribe, shall be considered as piracy, and that four months

from this date, all those of my people convicted of being concerned in such an act shall be punished as pirates.

Dated 10th Showal 1255 A. H., corresponding to the 17th December A.D. 1839.

SEAL OF SYUD BIN SULTAN

Aitchison, Vol. XI, pp. 299-300

In the fourth article of the Arabic version of the Moresby treaty of 1822 no mention was made of the obligation of the Sultan or his authorities to assist in the apprehension of British subjects engaged in the slave trade, although this obligation was distinctly specified in the English version. He was therefore urged to have the omission rectified by an addition to the Arabic text. He was, however, averse to alteration being made in the treaty; but in a separate letter, dated 18 August 1845, he bound himself, his heirs and authorities to afford assistance, when required by persons authorized to demand it, in apprehending British subjects engaged in the slave trade.

TRANSLATION of the annexed letter, dated 18th August 1845, from HIS HIGHNESS the IMAM of MUSCAT, to CAPTAIN HAMERTON, relative to the fourth Article of the TREATY concluded on the 10th September 1822 by CAPTAIN MORESBY with HIS HIGHNESS the IMAM of MUSCAT.

After Compliments. — Your excellent letter has reached, and your friend understood its contents; you mention that you have received a letter from the mighty Government, containing orders to you to bring to our notice that, in the 4th Article of the Treaty we concluded with Captain Moresby in the year 1822, it is mentioned in the English version that it is incumbent on us, and our heirs and Governors, to assist in apprehending English subjects engaged in the slave trade, but that such is not mentioned in the Arabic version of the treaty, and my friend (you) considering it not necessary to alter the Treaty, nevertheless we consider it incumbent on us, our heirs and Governors, that we should assist to apprehend English subjects who may be engaged in the slave trade. Therefore whoever may be accredited from the Government and require assistance from us, shall receive it accordingly. Whatever you may require let us know, and peace be on you.

Dated 4th Shaban 1241, 18th August 1845.

Aitchison, Vol. XI, p. 292.

In 1845 Said entered into a Treaty prohibiting from 1 January 1847 the export of slaves from his African dominions and their importation from any part of Africa into his dominions in Asia, and agreeing to use his influence with the Sheikhs of Arabia, the Red Sea and the Persian Gulf to put a stop to the slave trade. The treaty, however, did not prohibit the transport of slaves from one port to another in his African possessions.

AGREEMENT between HER MAJESTY the QUEEN of the UNITED KINGDOM of GREAT BRITAIN and IRELAND and HIS HIGHNESS SYUD SAEED BIN SULTAN, "the SULTAN of MUSCAT," for the termination of the EXPORT of SLAVES from the AFRICAN DOMINIONS of HIS HIGHNESS the SULTAN of MUSCAT, — 1845.

Her Majesty the Queen of the United Kingdom of Great Britain and Ireland being earnestly desirous that the export of slaves from the African dominions of His Highness the Sultan of Muscat should cease, and His Highness the Sultan of Muscat, in deference to the wishes of Her Majesty and of the British nation, and in furtherance of the dictates of humanity which have heretofore induced him to enter into engagement with Great Britain to restrict the export of slaves from his dominions, being willing to put an end to that trade, and Her Majesty the Queen of the United Kingdom of Great Britain and Ireland and His Highness the Sultan of Muscat having resolved to record with due form and solemnity this further restriction of the export of slaves, and Her Majesty having given due authority to Captain Hamerton, Her Representative at the Court of the Sultan of Muscat, to conclude an agreement with His Highness, accordingly His Highness Saeed Syud bin Sultan, for himself, his heirs and successors, and Captain Hamerton, on behalf of the Queen of the United Kingdom of Great Britain and Ireland, her heirs and successors, have agreed upon and concluded the following Articles: —

ARTICLE 1.

His Highness the Sultan of Muscat here engages to prohibit, under the severest penalties, the export of slaves from his African dominions, and to issue orders to his Officers to prevent and suppress such trade.

ARTICLE 2.

His Highness the Sultan of Muscat further engages to prohibit, under the severest penalties, the importation of slaves from any part of Africa into his possessions in Asia, and to use his utmost influence with all the Chiefs of Arabia, the Red Sea, and the Persian Gulf, in like manner, to prevent the introduction of slaves from Africa into their respective territories.

ARTICLE 3.

His Highness the Sultan of Muscat grants to the ships of Her Majesty's Navy as well as to those of the East India Company, permission to seize and confiscate any vessels, the property of His Highness or of his subjects, carrying on slave trade, excepting only such as are engaged in the transport of slaves from one port to another of his own dominions in Africa between the port of Lamoo to the north and its dependencies, the northern limit of which is the north point of Kuyhoor Island in 1° 57′ (one degree and fifty-seven minutes) South Latitude, and the port of Kulwa to the south and its dependencies, the southern limit of which is the Songa Manora or Pagoda Point in 9° 2′ (nine degrees and two minutes) South Latitude, including the Islands of Zanzibar, Pemba, and Monfea.

ARTICLE 4.

This agreement to commence and have effect from the 1st (first) day of January 1847 (one thousand eight hundred and forty-seven) of the year of Christ, and the 15th day of the month of Mahaneerun 1263 (twelve hundred and sixty-three) of the Hegira.

Done at Zanzibar this 2nd (second) day of October 1845 (one thousand eight hundred and forty-five) of the year of Christ and 29th day of Ramzan 1261 (twelve hundred and sixty-one) of the Hegira.

ATKINS HAMERTON,
Captain.

On behalf of Her Majesty the Queen of the United Kingdom of Great Britain and Ireland, her heirs and successors.

Aitchison, Vol. XI. pp. 300-1.

In consenting to this treaty Said requested that three additional articles might be added, prohibiting the search of his vessels in the limits within which the transport of slaves was allowed under the treaty, and of his vessels coming from the Arabian and Red Seas to Africa, and stipulating that if slaves were stolen from the Zanzibar territories he should not be held responsible. These articles do not appear to have been formally agreed to, but Said was informed in the name of Her Majesty's Government that British ships of war would search only such vessels under the Muscat flag as might reasonably be suspected of being engaged in the slave trade; that, therefore, the description of vessels mentioned in the articles would not be searched unless there should be good grounds for suspecting them to be so engaged; and that, in any case, if they should be searched and found not to be so engaged, that fact would be ascertained in a very short space of time, and they would not be prevented for more than a quarter or half an hour from continuing on their voyage.

Article three was assumed to have been the result of Said's concern lest the supply of Abyssinian concubines and African eunuchs from the Red Sea and Gulf of Tajurra be halted.

Additional Articles to the Agreement concluded on the 2nd October 1845, corresponding to the 29th Ramzan 1261 Hijira, proposed by His Highness the Imam of Muscat.

ARTICLE 1.

That no vessels belonging to His Highness Saiyid Said bin Sultan, the Imam of Muscat, or belonging to his subjects, be searched by English men-of-war between the boundary of Lamu to the north and Kilwa to the south, mentioned in the treaty concluded on the 2nd October 1845, corresponding with the 29th Ramzan 1261.

ARTICLE 2.

It may perhaps be reported to them (the British Government) that an individual has stolen slaves from the territories of Saiyid Said, the Sultan of Muscat, which are in Africa; unless this be proved, His Highness Saiyid, the Sultan of Muscat, shall not be called to account for it.

ARTICLE 3.

It is known that the vessels belonging to His Highness the Sultan of Muscat and those belonging to his subjects coming from the Arabian and Red Seas, do not bring slaves from those parts to the territories of the Sultan of Muscat which are in Africa, accordingly English men-of-war shall not search nor trouble them.

Aitchison Vol. XI. pp. 271-2

The following is an engagement prohibiting the importation of African slaves into Persia by sea.

TRANSLATION of a FIRMAN issued by HIS MAJESTY the SHAH to MIRZA NEBBEE KHAN, GOVERNOR of ISPAHAN and PERSIAN ARABIA, 1848.

To the high in rank, the superior of Generals, the esteemed of the sovereign, Mirza Nebbee Khan, Chief of the Civil Law Court and Governor of Ispahan and Arabia, who has been honoured by the favour of the pure mind of the king of kings, be it known that at this time the high in rank, the noble and exalted, possessed of dignity, the pillar of Christian nobles, the cream of the great men of Christendom, the undoubted well-wisher of the State, Colonel Farrant, Chargé d'Affaires of the exalted English Government, who enjoys the unbounded favour of His Majesty the Shah, whose resplendent mind is desirous to gratify him, made a friendly request on the part of the minister of that exalted government from the ministers of His Majesty the Shah, etc., etc., that, with a view to preserve the existing friendship between the two exalted States, a decree should be issued from the source of magnificence (the Shah) that hereafter the importation of the negro tribes by sea should be forbidden, and this traffic be abolished.

In consequence of this it is ordered and ordained that that high in rank after perusing this Firman, which is equal to a decree of fate, it will be incumbent on him to issue positive and strict injunctions to the whole of the dealers in slaves who trade by sea, that henceforth by sea alone the importation and exportation of negroes into the Persian dominions is entirely forbidden, but not by land. Not a single individual will be permitted to bring negroes by sea without being subjected to severe punishment.

That high in rank must in this matter give peremptory orders throughout his government and not be remiss.

Written in the month of Rejjeb, 1264—June 1848

Aitchinson, Vol. XIII, p. 75

CONVENTION concluded between COLONEL SHEIL and AMEER-E-NIZAM for the detention and search of PERSIAN VESSELS by BRITISH and EAST INDIA COMPANY'S CRUIZERS. – 1851.

The Persian Government agrees that the ships of war of the British Government and of the East India Company shall, in order to prevent the chance of negro slaves, male and female, being imported, be permitted for the period of eleven years to search Persian merchant vessels in the manner detailed in this document, with the exception of Persian Government vessels, not being vessels the property of merchants, or the property of Persian subjects; with those government vessels there is to be no interference whatever. The Persian Government agrees that in no manner whatever shall any negro slaves be imported in the vessels of the Persian Government.

Aitchison Vol. XIII. p. 76.

In October 1855 Britain entered into engagements with a number of tribes on the Somaliland coast for the suppression of the slave trade.

The following is the translation of an Agreement entered into on 14 October 1855 by the Owlakee chiefs for the Suppression of the Slave Trade. Similar engagements were entered into with the elders of the Habr Gerhagis and Habr Taljala tribes on 17 October 1855.

In the name of the Most Merciful God, and Him we implore! The reason for writing this bond is that influenced by motives of humanity and by a desire to conform to the principles on which the great English Government is conducted, we lend a willing ear to the proposals of our sincere friend Brigadier W.M. Coghlan, Governor of Aden, that we shall covenant with him and with each other to abolish and prohibit the exportation of slaves from any one part of Africa to any other place in Africa or Asia, or elsewhere under our authority.

We, whose names and seals are set to this Bond, do therefore in the sight of God and of man solemnly proclaim our intentions to prohibit the exportation of slaves from Africa by every means in our power; we will export none ourselves, nor will we permit our subjects to do so, and any vessel found carrying slaves shall be seized and confiscated and the slaves shall be released.

Aitchison Vol. XI. p. 106.

On 22 March 1868, the Sultan of Zanzibar issued a decree prohibiting the traffic in slaves between Kilwa and Lamu during the season of the north-east monsoon, 1 January to 15 May.

"In the name of God, the forgiving and the merciful. From him who is in the keeping of God, Majid bin Saeed. Be it known to all men, that all vessels proved to be carrying slaves during the monsoon, between the known limits of Kilwa and Lamoo, shall be burned: also all vessels in which there shall exist proof of their being fitted-out for the purpose of carrying slaves; an extra quantity of tanks and feed, and the presence of irons, shall be deemed to be sufficient proof to condemn the vessel.

2. Also all persons of our subjects proved to be engaged in the Slave Trade with the Coast of Arabia, shall be exiled from Zanzibar, and shall be further fined, for every Slave so exported, 10 dollars; and their property shall be sold, if necessary, to pay the said fine.

3. All persons concealing slaves for the northern Arabs, and others (from the Coast of Arabia) shall be fined, for every slave so concealed, 10 dollars; and their property shall be sold, if necessary, to pay the fine.

4. Whosoever shall give information regarding slaves having been hidden in houses occupied by Northern Arabs, shall receive 1 rupee for every slave so discovered; and whosoever shall give information of a vessel with slaves on board, shall receive 20 dollars on its being proved that such is the case.

5. Whosoever shall sell slaves to the Arabs other than our subjects shall be fined, for every slave so sold 20 dollars; and he shall be

further subjected to imprisonment in irons for two calendar months. Likewise auctioneers, unknown to the authorities, shall not sell slaves during the monsoon; and whosoever shall sell slaves contrary to the order of the Slave Bazaar Master shall be fined, for every slave so sold 5 dollars: and he shall further be punished with imprisonment in irons for two months. Also all auctioneers selling slaves during the monsoon, shall make a report of the number of slaves sold, their names, and the names of the purchasers, to the Slave Bazaar Master, so that he may be fined, for every slave so sold, 19 dollars; and they shall be further punished with two months imprisonment in irons. And, likewise, every person found to be buying more slaves in the monsoon than his means will warrant, and shall be reported by the auctioneers to the Government, who shall cause an inquiry to be made in the matter; and if the slaves so purchased are found to be in the possession of the said purchaser, or if they have been sold to our subjects, well and good, otherwise such individuals shall be fined; for every slave so purchased, 10 dollars; and they shall be subject to six months imprisonment in irons."

(Sealed) Majid Bin Saeed Bin, Sultan.

Dated 27th Dhelkaada, 1284. (March 22, 1868)

SP LVI 1868-69, No. 86. Incl. 2.

In May 1868, the Sultan addressed a letter to Sheikhs along the coast of Arabia, enclosing a copy of the above proclamation and notifying his intention of burning northern dhows violating it: 'they shall be burned forwith, as their sole business here is to steal children of the inhabitants of Zanzibar and their slaves'.

SP LVI 1868-69 No. 88 Incl. 1.

On 4 August 1877, a convention was signed by the representatives of Great Britain and Egypt, by which the latter country undertook the following engagements. This is extracted from *The Times*, 25 January 1878.

Public trading in slaves, whether negroes or Abyssinians, suppressed immediately. Their importation or exportation, whether by land or by sea, forbidden. Convicted traders to be held guilty of the crime of robbery with murder. Private sales or transfers between family and family to be abolished in Egypt in 1884; in the Soudan and other Egyptian dependencies in 1889. All dealings in white slaves to be abolished in 1884. Any person convicted of mutilation of children to be held guilty of the crime of murder. A special Trade Department to be formed in order to carry out the convention, secure the punishment of the offenders, and the future of the liberated slaves.

Captain Malcolm, R.N., lately sent by the British Government to assist Egypt in the suppression of the slave-trade in the Red Sea, has been made a Pasha, the fourth English Pasha in the Egyptian service. He left Suez last week on his mission with two vessels of the Egyptian Navy. He first proceeds to Massowah to concert a joint plan of action with Gordon Pasha, the Governor-General of the Soudan. The following decrees concerning the slave-trade were published in the *Moniteur* of last Saturday, and will all interest the English public: —

"We, Khedive of Egypt, whereas a Convention was signed at Alexandria, the 4th of August, 1877, between the Government of Great Britain and Ireland and my Government concerning the suppression of the slave-trade, have decreed and decree: —

"Art. 1. The transport of slaves on any ship whatever is forbidden, whether the slaves are sailors or passengers, whether they are intended to be sold or exchanged.

"Art. 2. Every vessel for the transport of slaves, having, for example, a deck set aside for this kind of transport, or having on board irons or water barrels more than sufficient for the crew and passengers, will be considered as intended for the slave-trade.

"Art. 3. The transit of slaves over Egyptian territory by land or sea, with the object of either sale or transfer, or any depôt of slaves in any part of the country, is also forbidden.

Art. 4. The Judges we shall name to carry out this law will have jurisdiction in whatever part of our territory they may be. They will have the power of naming any person as clerk to assist them.

"Art. 5. Whosoever is qualified to seize a ship, a slave depôt, or a slave gang, must, on making a seizure, place in the hands of the Judge a report under oath. If he is not in the Egyptian service he must point out in his report the article of the Slave Convention under which he has acted. The report must contain the names of the witnesses, the description of the ship, the nature of the cargo, the number of the crew, the number of the slaves and passengers.

"Art. 6. The Judge must summon before him, at a day and hour named, the person who has effected the seizure, the subject of seizure, the witnesses, and all persons who can give information. Notice of twenty-four hours as a *minimum*, and seven days as a *maximum* must be given from the date of the report under oath.

"Art. 7. The inquiry may (*sic*) be conducted orally.

"Art. 8. The sentence of the Judge shall be final, and transmitted by him to the Minister of Justice.

"Art. 9. The Judge shall have power to inflict the following sentences: 1. Confiscation of the ship, cargo, and slaves; 2. Fine of £20 as a *maximum*; 3. Three months' imprisonment as a *maximum*;

4. Payment of the costs as fixed by the Judge.

"Art. 10. The Judge shall have power to send the parties before the Minister of War.

"Art. 11. In the case of an arbitrary or unjust seizure, the person making the seizure may be ordered to pay to the injured party 50 centimes a day per ton, and an indemnity of 3 per cent on the value of the cargo, as valued by the Judge.

"*Cairo, Jan.* 1, 1878."   "ISMAIL."

This is followed by a second decree, which runs thus: —

"We, Khedive of Egypt, have decreed and decree, —

"Art. 1. A service is established for the suppression of the slave trade in the Red Sea, and on the coast which is under our rule.

"Art. 2. His Excellency Malcolm Pasha is appointed Director-General.

"Art. 3. Our Minister of Justice is charged with the execution of this Decree.

"*Cairo, Jan. 1.*"   "ISMAIL."

A third decree follows: —

"We, Khedive of Egypt, have decreed and decree: —

"His Excellency Malcolm Pasha, Director-General of the service for the suppression of the slave-trade in the Red Sea and on the coasts which are under rule, is appointed Judge, with the powers set forth in our decree of this day.

"*Cairo.*"   "ISMAIL."

Finally comes this notice: —

"By decree of His Highness the Khedive Captain George John Malcolm, of the British Navy, has been raised to the rank of General of Brigade."

Following the recovery of the Sudan, after the defeat of the Khalifa's forces in 1898, an agreement between the British Government and the Government of the Khedive of Egypt, relative to the administration of the Sudan and signed at Cairo on 19 January 1899, stated

The importation of slaves into the Soudan, as also their exportation, is absolutely prohibited. Provision shall be made by Proclamation for the enforcement of this Regulation.

CONVENTION BETWEEN GREAT BRITAIN AND PERSIA FOR THE
SUPPRESSION OF THE TRAFFIC IN SLAVES

Signed in the English and Persian languages, at Tehran, 2nd March
1882.

[*Ratifications exchanged at Tehran, 14th June* 1882.]

In the name of God, the Almighty, All-Merciful

HER MAJESTY the Queen of the United Kingdom of Great Britain
and Ireland, Empress of India, and His Majesty the Shah of Persia,
being mutually animated by a sincere desire to co-operate for the
extinction of the barbarous Traffic in Slaves, have resolved to
conclude a Convention for the purpose of attaining this object, and
have named as their Plenipotentiaries, that is to say:

Her Majesty the Queen of the United Kingdom of Great Britain
and Ireland, Empress of India — Roland Ferguson
Thomson, Esquire, Her Envoy Extraordinary and Minister
Plenipoteniary at the Court of Persia;

And His Majesty the Shah of Persia — His Excellency Mirza
Saeed Khan, His Minister for Foreign Affairs;

Who, after having communicated to each other their full powers,
found in good and due form, have agreed upon and concluded the
following Articles: —

ARTICLE 1.

*Permission to British Cruizers to visit and detain Persian Merchant
Vessels.*

In order to prevent the chance of negro slaves, male and female,
being imported into Persia, British cruizers shall be permitted to visit
and detain merchant vessels under the Persian flag, or belonging to
Persian subjects, which may be engaged in, or which there may be
reasonable grounds for suspecting to be or to have been engaged
during the voyage on which they are met, in carrying slaves; and if
any such slaves are found on board such merchant vessels, the vessel,
with all on board, shall be taken before the nearest Persian
authorities for trial.

*Persons provided with Government Passports not to be molested
under certain circumstances.*

But no person whatsoever who, being furnished with a
Government passport, countersigned by a British Resident or Consul,
may have gone from Persia to visit the places of pilgrimage, shall,

when returning, be interfered with, provided such a person be not accompanied by more negroes, either male or female, than the number mentioned in his original pass. The presence of any such additional negro or negroes shall be *prima facie* evidence of an attempted Traffic in Slaves.

ARTICLE 2.

British Officer to be present at adjudication of captured Vessels.

If any merchant vessel under the Persian flag be captured by a British cruizer and taken into a Persian port for adjudication, it shall be the officer of the British cruizer making the capture, or some duly authorized officer of the British Government, who shall be present at such adjudication.

Disposal of condemned Vessels and Slaves found on board.

In the event of the captured merchant vessel being condemned and sold, the proceeds of such sale shall go to the Persian Government, and all slaves found on board such a vessel shall be handed over to the British authorities.

ARTICLE 3.

Persians engaging in Slave Traffic by Sea to be severely punished.

His Majesty the Shah of Persia agrees to punish severely all Persian subjects or foreigners amenable to Persian jurisdiction who may be found engaging in Slave Traffic by sea.

Slaves imported to be manumitted and protected.

And to manumit and guarantee the safety and proper treatment of all slaves illegally imported, that is to say, imported by sea into His Majesty's dominions after the signature of the present convention.

ARTICLE 4.

Agreement of August 1851 cancelled.

The present convention shall come into operation on the 1st May 1882. After the convention shall so have been brought into operation, Article XIII of the Treaty between Great Britain and Persia, signed at Paris on the 4th March 1857 (page 81), by which the Agreement entered into by Great Britain and Persia in August 1851 (page 76) was renewed, shall be considered as cancelled, except as to any proceeding that may have already been taken or commenced in virtue thereof.

ARTICLE 5.

The ratifications of the present convention shall be exchanged at

Tehran within five months, or sooner if practicable.

Done at Tehran, in quadruplicate, this 2nd day of the month of March, in the year of Our Lord 1882.

RONALD F. THOMSON.

MIRZA SAEED KHAN.

Aitchison, Vol XIII, pp. 87-8.

TREATY BETWEEN HER MAJESTY AND HIS MAJESTY THE KING OF ABYSSINIA FOR THE SUPPRESSION OF THE SLAVE TRADE.

Signed at Adowa, June 3, 1884.

[*Ratified by Her Majesty, July 12, 1884.*]

Her Majesty the Queen of the United Kingdom of Great Britain and Ireland, Empress of India, and His Majesty Johannis, made by the Almighty King of Sion, Negoosa Negust of Ethiopia and its dependencies, being desirous of prohibiting and perpetually abolishing the Slave Trade, they have agreed to conclude a Treaty for this purpose, which shall be binding on themselves, their heirs, and successors; and to that end Rear-Admiral Sir William Hewett, Commander-in-Chief of Her Majesty's ships of war in the East Indies, acting on the behalf of Her Majesty the Queen of Great Britain and Ireland, Empress of India, and His Majesty Johannis, Negoosa Negust of Ethiopia, acting on his own behalf, they have agreed upon and concluded the following Articles: —

Article 1.

His Majesty the Negoosa Negust agrees to prohibit and to prevent, to the best of his ability, the buying and selling of slaves within his dominions.

Article II.

His Majesty the Negoosa Negust agrees to prohibit and to prevent, to the best of his ability, the import or export of slaves to or from his dominions.

Article III.

His majesty the Negoosa Negust engages to protect, to the utmost of his power, all liberated slaves, and to punish severely any attempt to molest them, or to reduce them again to slavery.

Article IV

Her Britannic Majesty has made Treaties with many foreign States, by which it is permitted to her officers to seize all ships belonging to such foreign States engaged in the transport or conveyance of slaves upon the sea; and Her Majesty engages to liberate any subjects of His Majesty the Negoosa Negust who may be found detained as slaves in any ship captured by the officers of Her Majesty, and to take steps to send such subjects back to the dominions of His Majesty the Negoosa Negust.

Article V.

The present Treaty shall be ratified, and the ratification shall be forwarded to Adowa as soon as possible.

In witness whereof, Rear-Admiral Sir William Hewett, on the behalf of her Majesty the Queen of Great Britain and Ireland, Empress of India, and Johannis, Negoosa Negust of Ethiopia, on his own behalf, have signed the same, and (or) have affixed their seals to this Treaty, made at Adowa the 3rd day of June, 1884, corresponding to the 27th day of Goonvet, 1876.

(L.S.) (Seal of the King of Abysinnia.)

(L. S.) W. HEWETT.

N.B. — We have had no representative at Massowah to carry out this Treaty.

The following appeared in the *Anti-Slavery Reporter* Vol. IX. Fourth Series, November–December 1889.

Law for the repression of the Negro Slave-Trade in the Ottoman Empire, sanctioned by Imperial Iradé: — 16 Dec. 1889

Art. 1. The commerce, entry, and passage of black Slaves in the Ottoman Empire and its dependencies is prohibited.

Art. 2. Black Slaves, going abroad as domestic servants with their masters or mistresses, and those employed as sailors on board trading vessels, are excepted from this prohibition. Masters and mistresses of Slaves must, however, exhibit a certificate showing their age and their personal appearance and the nature of their employment. The age, personal description, and employment of Slaves serving as sailors on board merchant vessels shall be entered on the ship's register.

Art. 3. Failing such certificates or entries the Slaves shall be considered free; the tribunal, or, where none exists, the local government, will grant them certificates of manumission. Their owners, in default of proof to the contrary, shall be considered as traders in Slaves.

Art. 4. Manumitted Slaves going out of the Ottoman Empire will receive a passport, declaring them to be free. Only in the official documents delivered for Slaves accompanying their proprietors, as set forth in Article 3, age, personal appearance, and quality will be stated.

Art. 5. Persons who, contrary to the prohibition in Article I, engage directly or indirectly in Slave-trade, persons who assist in that trade, or captains of ships carrying Slaves, will be condemned for the first offence to a year's imprisonment, and to double that term for a repetition of the offence. The Slaves found in their possession will be confiscated, and, as prescribed in Article 3, certificates of manumission will be delivered to them.

Art. 6. If any children are found among the Slaves, the persons engaged in the traffic, as well as those who have mutilated them or been guilty of other unlawful practices, will be liable to the penalties ordained by the penal code, in addition to those prescribed in Article 5.

Art. 7. If, in any part of the Empire crimes mentioned in Article 6, such as mutilation, or traffic in negro children, are committed, the local civil functionaries where those crimes are committed will, in the limits of their jurisdiction, arrest the culprits, draw up a process verbal of the preliminary inquiry, and will send them and the documents concerning the case to a competent tribunal.

Art. 8. In virtue of the treaty concluded between the Imperial Ottoman Government and the British Government, on the 11th Rebi-ul-Akhir, 1297, the warships of the two States will seize and confiscate with all their contents every vessel, whether under Ottoman or British flag, carrying negro Slaves. If the vessels seized by Ottoman war-ships are British, they will be delivered to the British Government in order that the legal prescriptions may be applied, and the promised reward paid. On the other hand the Ottoman vessels captured by the respective war-ships of the contracting Powers shall be delivered to the Ottoman Government, by whom the reward will be given.

Art. 9. When a Slave-carrying ship is seized and handed over to the Ottoman Government, the owner, or if he resides in a foreign country, the captain, will be judicially condemned to pay a fine of five Turkish pounds for each Slave. This sum shall be made over by way of reward to the officers and crew of the vessel effecting the seizure. Judicial costs shall be exacted separately. If the owner or captain of the seized vessel refuse to pay such fine and costs, a part or the whole of the contents of the ship, other than its cargo of Slaves, and in case of need the vessel itself, shall be sold by public auction. After deduction from the proceeds of the sale of the judicial costs and the reward, the balance will be handed over to the owner. Judgments in such cases are not subject to appeal.

Art. 10. In the legal proceedings relating to the negro Slave-trade, the public prosecutors will perform the duties attaching to their attributions, and the captain of the ship which has seized the Slave-carrying vessel will appear as a party in the action.

Given the 22 Rebi-ul-Akhir, 1307.

The General Act of the Brussels Conference of July 1890, in its articles relating to the slave trade, has been termed the Magna Carta of the African slave trade. The wide-ranging measures for action against the slave trade which were provided for by the Conference represent the concerted attempt by the Great Powers to eradicate the traffic from Africa, and more especially Eastern Africa, its last stronghold. For the first time also, at an international level, we see an open declaration against the making of eunuchs.

The Contracting Powers undertake, unless this has already been provided for by laws in accordance with the spirit of the present Article, to enact or propose to their respective Legislatures, in the course of one year at latest from the date of the signature of the present General Act, a Law applying, on the one hand, the provisions of their penal laws concerning grave offences against the person, to the organizers and abettors of manhunts, to perpetrators of the mutilation of adults and male infants, and to all persons who may take part in the capture of slaves by violence;

The series of decrees commencing with the Moresby treaty of 1822 and the Hamerton treaty of 1845, to end the slave trade and slavery in the Sultan of Zanzibar's dominions, continued throughout the remainder of the century. Although there were a number of proclamations, the major landmarks were the decrees of 1873, 1890 and 1897.

The 1873 treaty was meant to end the slave trade at sea between different parts of the Sultan's African dominions, and to close the slave markets, especially that at Zanzibar. A separate proclamation by the Sultan forbade the fitting out of caravans for slaving in the interior.

The signing of the 1873 treaty was followed by a proclamation from Sultan Barghash as follows: —

To all our subjects who may see this, and also to others, May God save you, Now that we have prohibited the transport of raw slaves by sea in all our harbours and have closed the markets which are for the sale of slaves throughout all our dominions. Whosoever, therefore, shall ship a raw slave after this date, will render himself liable to punishment, and this he will bring upon himself. Be this known.

June 8th 1873.

The 1873 treaty did not achieve the desired effect in ending the slave trade. There were manifold ways of evading it. Slaves continued to be shipped under the guise of domestic slaves, servants, ship's crew, and as wives of the Arabs. In addition, there was much smuggling of slaves, and running them under the protection of the French flag which gave immunity from search by British cruisers.

The 1890 decree sought to end the traffic in slaves of all description.

Proclamation

In the name of God the Merciful, the Compassionate, the following Decree is published by us, Seyyid Ali-bin Saïd, Sultan of Zanzibar, and is to be made known to, and obeyed by, all our subjects within our dominions from this date

Decree.

1. We hereby confirm all former Decrees and Ordinances made by our predecessors against slavery and the Slave Trade, and declare that, whether such Decrees have hitherto been put in force or not, they shall for the future be binding on ourselves and on our subjects.

2. We declare that, subject to the conditions stated below, all slaves lawfully possessed on this date by our subjects shall remain with their owners as at present. Their status shall be unchanged.

3. We absolutely prohibit from this date all exchange, sale, or purchase of slaves, domestic or otherwise. There shall be no more traffic whatever in slaves of any description. Any houses heretofore kept for traffic in domestic slaves by slave-brokers shall be for ever closed, and any person found acting as a broker for the exchange or sale of slaves shall be liable under our orders to severe punishment, and to be deported from our dominions. Any Arab or other of our subjects hereafter found exchanging, purchasing, obtaining, or selling domestic or other slaves shall be liable under our orders to severe punishment, to deportation, and the forfeiture of all his slaves. Any house in which traffic of any kind in any description of slave may take place shall be forfeited.

4. Slaves may be inherited at the death of their owner only by the lawful children of the deceased. If the owner leaves no such children, his slaves shall, *ipso facto*, become free on the death of their owner.

5. Any Arab or other of our subjects who shall habitually ill-treat his slave, or shall be found in the possession of new slaves, shall be liable under our orders to severe punishment, and in flagrant cases of cruelty to the forfeiture of all his slaves.

6. Such of our subjects as may marry persons subject to British jurisdiction, as well as the issue of all such marriages, are hereby disabled from holding slaves, and all slaves of such of our subjects as are already so married are now declared to be free.

7. All our subjects who, once slaves, have been freed by British authority, or who have long since been freed by persons subject to British jurisdiction, are hereby disabled from owning slaves, and all slaves of such persons are now declared to be free.

All slaves who, after the date of this Decree, may lawfully obtain their freedom are for every disqualified from holding slaves, under pain of severe punishment.

8. Every slave shall be entitled as a right at any time henceforth to purchase his freedom at a just and reasonable tariff, to be fixed by ourselves and our Arab subjects. The purchase-money, on our order, shall be paid by the slave to his owner before a Kadi, who shall at once furnish the slave with a paper of freedom, and such freed slaves shall receive our special protection against ill-treatment. This protection shall also be specially extended to all slaves who may gain their freedom under any of the provisions of this Decree.

9. From the date of this Decree every slave shall have the same right as any of our other subjects who are not slaves to bring and prosecute any complaints or claims before our Kadis.

Given under our hand this 15th day of El Haj, 1307, at Zanzibar (1st August, 1890).

(Signed)   ALI-BIN-SAID,

Sultan of Zanzibar.

The Sultan of Zanzibar, following the issuing of the decree of 1 August 1890, had second thoughts on the matter. Under that decree, by article 8, slaves were entitled to purchase their freedom. Fearful lest slaves might look upon this as an encouragement to run away to earn money to purchase their freedom, the Sultan quickly followed up the decree with the two following proclamations.

Proclamation.

Be it known to all our subjects that our Decree of the 15th El Haj, this year 1307, which is now in force, and must remain in force, shall not be the cause of bad behaviour or disobedience on the part of the lawful slaves towards their masters.

Be it known to all that slaves who shall run away without just cause or otherwise behave badly, shall be punished as before, according to justice, and, if necessary, they shall be brought before us for punishment.

Let this be known to everybody.

Signed and sealed at Zanzibar the 23rd El Haj, 1307 (9the August, 1890).

(Signed)   ALI-BIN-SAID.

Proclamation.

Be it known to all men our subjects, with reference to what I wrote on the 15th Haj (1st August), and put up in the Custom-house.

If any slave runs away from his master, or does anything wrong, punish him as before. If any slave does great wrong, kills any one, or steals, send him to the Liwali, who will punish him. You will see it and be pleased.

If any slave brings money to the Kadi to purchase his freedom, his master will not be forced to take the money.

(Signed)   SEYYID ALI-BIN-SAID.

Zanzibar, 3 Moharrum, 1307 (*20th August,* 1890).

The *Zanzibar Gazette* of 7 April 1897 published the following.

DECREE DATED 1ST OF ZILKADA, 1314.

(Translation)

From Seyyid Hamoud-bin-Mahomed-bin-Said to all his subjects:

Whereas by a Treaty concluded in 1290 between her Majesty the Queen of England and His Highness the late Seyyid Barghash etc., the importation of slaves into the Islands of Zanzibar and Pemba was forbidden and declared to be illegal.

And whereas, owing to the lapse of years and other causes, the number of slaves legally imported and held in these islands has greatly decreased, so that many estates have gone out of cultivation.

And whereas the present system of slavery deters free labourers from coming to Our islands to take the place of those who have from death or other causes, disappeared, to the detriment of agriculture and of Our subjects, who are thus driven to borrow money at high interest against the Law of Islam and their own welfare, both of which are the objects of Our deepest solicitude.

And whereas the Apostle Mahomed (may God grant him blessings and peace!) has set before us as most praiseworthy the liberation of slaves, and We are Ourselves desirous of following his precepts, and of encouraging the introduction of free labour.

And whereas our Late predecessor, Seyyid Ali, in the Decree in which he forbade for the future the sale of slaves or their transmission except by direct inheritance, declared that, subject to the conditions stated in that Decree, all slaves lawfully possessed on that date by his subjects should remain with their owners, and that their status should be unchanged, so that it would not be equitable to deprive them of any rights enjoyed under that Decree without awarding compensation to their present possessors.

We, therefore, having considered this question most carefully in all its aspects, and having in view the benefiting of all classes of Our faithful subjects have decided, with the advice of Our First Minister, to promulgate, and We do hereby promulgate the following Decree:-

ARTICLE 1. From and after this 1st day of Zilkada, all claims of whatever description made before any Court or public authority in respect of the alleged relations of master and slave shall be referred to the District Court (Mehkemet-el-Wilaya) within whose jurisdiction they may arise, and shall be cognizable by that Court alone.

ARTICLE 2. From and after this 1st day of Zilkada the District Court shall decline to enforce any alleged rights over the body, service, or property of any person on the ground that such person is a slave, but wherever any person shall claim that he was lawfully possessed of such rights, in accordance with the Decrees of Our predecessors, before the publication of the present Decree, and has now by the application of the said Decree been deprived of them, and has suffered loss by such deprivation, then the Court, unless satisfied that the claim is unfounded, shall report to Our First Minister that it deems the claimant entitled, in consideration of the loss of such rights and damage resulting therefrom, to such pecuniary compensation as may be a just and reasonable equivalent for their value, and Our First Minister shall then award to him such sum.

ARTICLE 3. The compensation money thus awarded shall not be liable to be claimed in respect of any debt for which the person of the slave for whom it was granted could not previously by law be seized.

ARTICLE 4. Any person whose right to freedom shall have been formally recognized under the 2nd Article shall be liable to any tax, abatement, corvee, or payment in lieu of corvee, which Our Government may at any time hereafter see fit to impose on the general body of its subjects, and shall be bound, on pain of being declared a vagrant, to show that he possesses a regular domicile and means of subsistence, and where such domicile is situated on land owned by any other person, to pay to the owner of such land such rent (which may take the form of an equivalent in labour or produce) as may be agreed upon between them before the District Court.

ARTICLE 5. Concubines shall be regarded as inmates of the Harem in the same sense as wives, and shall remain in their present relations unless they should demand their dissolution on the ground of cruelty, in which case the District Court shall grant it if the alleged cruelty has been proved to its satisfaction. A concubine not having borne children may be redeemed with the sanction of the Court.

ARTICLE 6. Any person making any claim under any of the provisions of this Decree, shall have the right to appeal from the decision of the District Court to Ourselves, or to such Judge or other public authority as We may from time to time see fit to delegate for the purpose.

Written by his order by his slave, Salim-bin-Mohamed.

(*Signed*)   HAMOUD-BIN-MAHOMED-BIN-SAID.

The decree of 1 April 1897, although generally assumed to have ended the status of slavery in Zanzibar and Pemba, left the responsibility for claiming freedom with the slave; formal application had to be made for issue of freedom papers, they did not come automatically. Nor was the status of concubines changed under the decree; they could not attain their freedom except under special circumstances, as on grounds of cruelty. Thus the effects of the 1897 decree worked themselves out slowly. Out of a total slave population in Zanzibar and Pemba of 100,000 in 1897, there were still 53,000 in slavery at the end of 1901. And of the remaining 47,000 only a small proportion were emancipated under the decree. Details are as follows:-

Freed (under the decree) ...	12-13,000	
Died-ordinary deaths......	10,000	
Died-small pox	20,000	
Disappeared	5,000	(possibly kidnapped, or to German territory and mainland as porters)
	47,000	

An official report in February 1902, from Mr B. S. Cave, British Consul at Zanzibar, to the Marquess of Lansdowne, stated

the rush for freedom which took place when the Decree first became known has apparently expended itself, the slaves who had real cause for complaint or real longings for emancipation, as well as those who were attracted by a sense of novelty or by visions of idleness and indulgence, have had their desires satisfied, and the remainder have made up their minds that it is better to remain as they are in comparative peace and contentment than to tempt Providence in some new and untried form.

FOCP 7946/158, 21 February 1902

The legal status of slavery was not abolished in the mainland coastal strip (leased from the Sultan by the British) until 1907. The last day of 1911 was fixed as the day on which no further claims for compensation to owners of slaves would be considered. And this date may be taken as the termination of the institution of slavery in British East africa. Mr J. P. Farler, who had for many years worked as a missionary in the Universities Mission to Central Africa, and had been Archdeacon of Magila before his retirement from the Mission owing to ill health, was later appointed as Commissioner for Pemba. He gives an explanation in his Slavery Report as to why there was no great rush by the slaves of Pemba to gain their freedom under the abolition decree of 1897.

There are one or two points on which there seems to be a misconception at home. First, I notice that at anti-slavery meetings there is generally a good deal of indignant protest against even the name of slavery continuing in Zanzibar or Pemba under the British flag. Now, the British flag is not flown in Zanzibar or Pemba; we are under the Sultan's flag. This country is not a British Colony, but a Mahommedan Sultanate under British protection, in which by Treaty the rights, customs, and laws of the people are to be maintained and guaranteed by the British Government. Some abolitionists may say: Why, then, continue our protection to a country where the name of slave is allowed to exist? — because there are other nations quite ready to assume the Protectorate if we give it up, who have no wish to abolish slavery at all in these countries. Are these good people desirous that this change should take place?

There is another misconception I should like to set right, that is, about the feeling of degradation at being a slave. There is no doubt but that the institution of slavery in any country does degrade, not only the slaves, but also the slave owners. But the slaves themselves do not feel any degradation in being called a slave. The word "slave" has a very different meaning in Swahili from what it has in English, and there is no stigma attached to it.

The Swahili word "mtumwa" (slave) is derived from the verb "kutuma," to send. The title of "Mohamed the Apostle of God" is "Mtume" (i.e., the one sent). It has exactly the same meaning as our word Apostle; while "mtumwa" (slave) is merely one who can be sent. So you see what an honourable connection the word has. The greatest Arabs, in writing to the Sultan, always sign themselves "Your slave," so and so. In many parts of the country, especially the mainland coast tribes, the word "Mtume" is frequently used for the Supreme Being.

The household slaves in large families are most scornful towards slaves freed by the Government; will hold no intercourse with them, and call them "Mateka," or, the spoils of the enemy: and this is a deadly insult. As mission boys walk about, they are frequently called after, "Mateka!"

FOCP 7946, Part LXVIII, Inclosure 2 in No. 158, 21 February 1902

Payment of compensation to owners of slaves under the 1897 decree led to many instances of fraud, as Brigadier-General A. E. Raikes, Acting First Minister at Zanzibar, retails in a despatch to Mr Cave in December 1902.

Many cases have been discovered by Arabs and others bringing up slaves for freedom, getting their compensation, and afterwards it has been discovered that the slaves were either not the slaves of the persons presenting them for freedom or not slaves at all.

Many slaves have been freed twice; many mainland people have come for freedom not being slaves. These frauds are most difficult to discover, as the slaves are coached up and witnesses are brought all telling the same story.

Again, another method they indulge in, is immediately they hear that a new official is writing their freedom, the already freed slaves come up again under a new name and with a new master on the understanding that if compensation is paid the supposed slave is to receive a portion of it.

From time to time, since the Decree, cases of fraud have been discovered, but it has never been so common as it has become now.

There are cases being found out every day, and we have in gaol at the present moment no less than eight masters, for freeing slaves fraudulently, and two cases under trial and others in view.

FOCP 8098/112, 10 December 1902

Officials in German East Africa tended to regard slavery dispassionately. The Germans made a clear distinction between domestic slavery and what they termed the 'raw' slave trade. Domestic slavery meant stability, good order, and an available labour supply: the 'raw' slave trade meant disruption of law and good order, and had to be suppressed rigorously. The intention of the following decree was to bring about a process of gradual extinction of slavery – a process which, if uninterrupted, would have taken as long as 1930 to 1940 to achieve; but as a result of World War I was terminated by the British when they took over German East Africa as a mandate in 1922.

DECREE RESPECTING DOMESTIC SLAVERY IN GERMAN EAST AFRICA

NOVEMBER 29, 1901

(*Translation*)

I

No one shall be placed in a condition of slavery, when he is not already in such, by disposing of himself by sale or by being sold by relations, or on account of debts or other obligations, or as punishment for adultery.

II

Every domestic slave is empowered to bring about a termination of his slavery by paying a ransom.

III

The amount of this ransom will be fixed by the competent authorities, and a document establishing his liberty is to be made out for every slave by the authorities, after the stipulated sum of money has been paid in.

IV

Every domestic slave must be permitted to work on his own account during two days of the week, or else to apply to his own uses the same proportion of the earnings of his work. So far as the rights fixed by custom in this respect are more favourable to the slave than this present Regulation, they are to remain unaltered. In case of a dispute between owner and slave on this point as on others, the matter will be decided by the competent authorities.

V

The owner of a domestic slave is bound also to support him in old age, and to care for him during illness. This obligation is not abolished when a slave, from incapacity of old age or illness, is given his freedom.

VI

The transference of rights of ownership over a domestic slave can only take place with the consent of the slave and before the competent authorities, on whose concurrence the transaction depends. Before allowing the transference, the authorities must examine the legality of the state of slavery, besides other points, which may appear to them as important, and especially pay attention to preventing the members of one family from being separated from one another without their consent.

VII

The right of ownership over a domestic slave is forfeited when the owner is guilty of a grave lack of duty towards his slave. The competent authorities must make official inquiries into any cases of this kind which may reach their ears, and are empowered to cause the slave to be set at liberty by means of a document declaratory of his freedom, without the ex-owner having the right to put in any claim to compensation.

VIII

Infractions of the Regulations laid down in the present Decree are punishable by a money fine of up to 500 rupees, or up to three months' imprisonment – that is, as far as higher punishments are not incurred under existing laws on the subject.

IX

This Decree comes into force on the day of its promulgation.

THE IMPERIAL CHANCELLOR,
(*Signed*) Count v. Bulow.

Berlin, November 29, 1901.

FOCP 7946/26, Inclosure, 1902

The last territory in eastern Africa to legislate against the slave trade was Abyssinia (Ethiopia). The following letter to the Marquess of Lansdowne from a British official, G. R. Clerk, at the court of the ruler of Abyssinia, indicates the grave reservations that remained in European minds as to anything coming from pronouncements by the ruler of Abyssinia, so addicted to slaving were the Abyssinians.

ADDIS ABABA,
September 7, 1903.

My Lord,

I have the honour to transmit to your Lordship herewith a translation of a notice issued by the Emperor Menelik on the 20th August last, renewing the prohibition of all dealing in slaves. This notice was published by being cried in the market-place of Addis Ababa and I have had some difficulty in obtaining the exact text. Its publication is due to representations made to the Emperor some time ago by the Italian Minister, and its intention is to prove to the European Legations here, and, through them, to their Governments, His Majesty's determination to conform with the terms of the Brussels Act. But as a deterrent to the traffic in slaves it is absolutely valueless, a fact which is admitted by every Abyssinian.

The demand for slaves in Addis Ababa is principally met in the following way. A soldier from Kaffa or Wallamo (the two provinces where slaves are most easily come by) gets leave to go to Addis Ababa with two or three servants. On arrival at the capital he soon finds where he can best dispose of them. He then offers them as a gift to the would-be-owner: the latter accepts them and in return, presses a gift of so many dollars on his 'friend'. These preliminaries are kept secret. A day or two later, the soldier pays a formal visit to the purchaser, accompanied by his servants and some witnesses. He then explains that he has been suddenly recalled to his post, that his servants will delay him, and that therefore, he will be very grateful if his friend will keep them in his house until he returns to claim them, an event which never happens. There is no scrutiny over soldiers going back to duty, and consequently his return to his garrison without his servants causes no official comment.

PROCLAMATION (*Translation*)

Regarding the Galla slave question; before now I wrote letters to all the districts; proclaimed proclamations and ex-communicated; but you still persist in stealing the Gallas and selling them for slaves. But hereafter whosoever I shall find selling Gallas, I shall not only punish him with his property but shall also give him a bodily punishment.

FOCP 8235, Part IX, No. 146, 7 September 1903

As valedictory to this collection of documents one might well quote the words of a person with long residence in Zanzibar in the earlier half of the twentieth century, L. W. Hollingsworth in *Zanzibar Under the Foreign Office 1890-1913*, London, 1953, pp. 158-9.

By the opening years of the twentieth century the long fight against slavery in the Sultan's dominions was at last brought to a successful conclusion. Moreover, with the complete abolition of domestic slavery, the Arab slave trade in East Africa was also dealt its death-blow. The natives of East and Central Africa had now no longer any cause to fear the swoop of armed slavers on their villages, the dreadful march in chains and yokes to the coast, and the journey in an overcrowded, foul-smelling dhow to Zanzibar. For deliverance from these horrors they had every reason to be grateful to their European emancipators.

It is less easy to assess what the African gained from the abolition of domestic slavery in the dominions of the Sultan. If he were fortunate enough to survive the rigours of the journey from the interior, the average slave was probably not very unhappy, once he had been set to work on a plantation in Zanzibar or Pemba. Although there were inevitably some cases of gross cruelty towards slaves, there seems little doubt that the average Zanzibar Arab was too easy-going to make a hard task-master. His estates were run in a patriarchal manner, the slaves being treated as inferior members of the family, rather than as mere chattels. Some writers have argued that after emancipation the African became a wage-slave, especially if he worked for a European employer, and it has even been asserted that many freed slaves preferred their former Arab masters to their new European employers, who exacted harder service and failed to treat them as fellow human beings. It is probably true that the slave felt that his Arab master, who was often the son of a negro concubine, was less removed from him racially than the white man. Hardinge pointed out that it was therefore natural that the African slave should prefer his Arab owner to the 'white alien conqueror', who, even if he had emancipated him, yet treated him as an inferior and was often 'a far more exacting taskmaster'. Whatever truth there may be in such arguments, there can be no doubt as to the honesty of purpose which inspired the great body of British humanitarian opinion in its resolute, if sometimes inept, struggles to destroy the evils of slavery and the slave trade wherever they flourished.

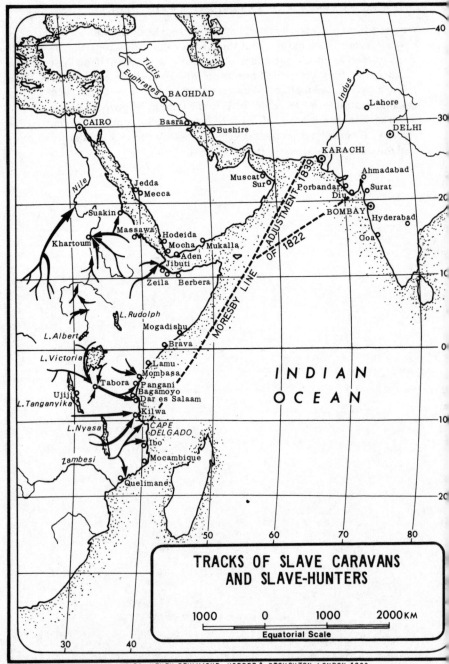

TRACKS OF SLAVE CARAVANS
AND SLAVE-HUNTERS

1000   0   1000   2000 KM

Equatorial Scale

ADAPTED FROM <u>TROPICAL AFRICA</u>, HENRY DRUMMOND, HODDER & STOUGHTON, LONDON, 1888

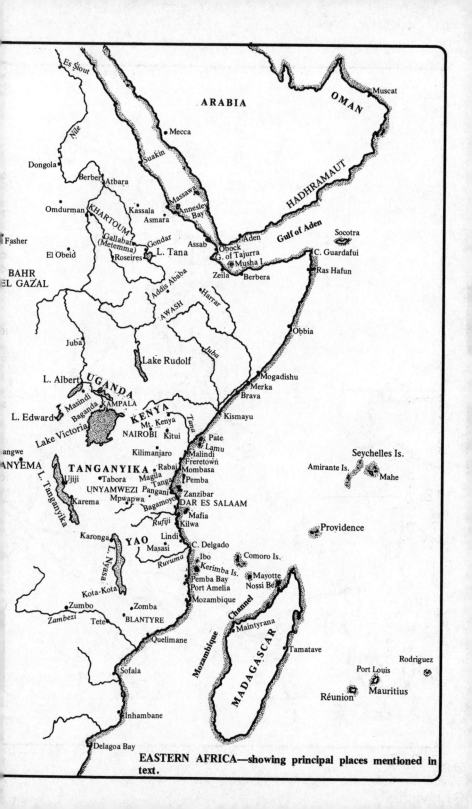

EASTERN AFRICA—showing principal places mentioned in text.

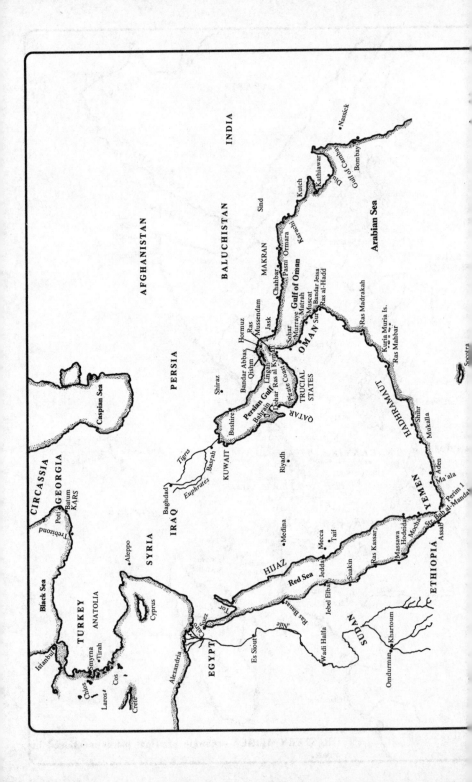

INDEX

Madagascar, 20, 23, 85, 98, 105
Mafia (Momfia), 20, 110
Magila, 128
Mahdism, 76
Majid, Sultan, 113
Makololo, 24-5
Malcolm, Captain G. J., 115
Manyuema, 23, 28, 29
Masai, 23, 30
Masailand, 41
Massawa, 59, 73
Mathews, Sir Lloyd (General), 31
Mauritius, 7, 103, 105
Mbe, 30
Mecca, 43, 62, 66, 68, 77, 79
Mehemet Ali, 55
Menelik, King, 65
Mersa Halaib, 71
Metemma (Matamma), (see Gallabat)
Middle East, xi, 31, 77
Mocha, 43
Mofio, King, 54
Mohilla, 85
Mokha Point, 94
Mombasa, xi, 31
Moncrief, Consul, 74
Mongallo River, 5
Moresby, Captain F., 103, 106-7
Morice, M., 4
Morocco, 66, 68
Mozambique, 4, 5, 7, 81
Muscat, xi, 10, 22, 85, 89, 100, 103,
    105-11
Mussalemia, 55

Ngoni, 23, 30
Niam-niam, 47-9, 54-5
Nile, The, 53, 55
Nooba, 55
Nossi Bé (Hellville), 98, 101
Nubia, ix, 45
Nubians, 48, 50, 52
Nyasa Lake, 16, 20, 23, 30

Obok, 98
Oldfield, Captain R. B., 91-2
Oman, ix, 2-3, 18, 101
Omani, xi, 10, 103
Opone, 1
Owen, Captain W. F. W., 4, 5, 18, 31,
    81
Owlakee, chiefs, 112

Pagoda Point, 110
Palmerston, Lord, 19, 77
Pasni, 107
Pearl diving, 80
Peel, Captain W., 44
Pemba, 28, 40-1, 90-1, 96, 110, 125-6,
    128, 132
Perim Island, 94
Periplus, The, ix, 1
Persia, 18, 20-1, 52, 62, 77, 85, 111-
    12, 116-19
Persian Gulf, xii, 1, 10, 80, 85, 89, 101,
    103, 107, 109
Pirate Coast, 103
Playfair, Colonel R. L., 98
Portal, Sir Gerald, 40
Portuguese, x, xi, 4, 23, 27
Prideaux, Captain W. F., 27, 96
Punt, Land of, ix

Quelimane, 4-6

Rabegh, 79
Raikes, Brigadier A. E., 129
Raouf Pasha, 58
Ras Hafun, 1
Ras Muteinah, 94
Red Sea, 10, 18, 23, 53, 55, 58-62, 68-
    71, 74, 95, 109-11, 116
Redwan Pasha, 71-2
Réunion, 101
Rigby, General C. P., 23, 101
Rio de Janeiro, 5
Rodd, R., 101
Rosebery, Lord, 101
Rossit, 71
Russell, Earl, 91
Russia, 77-8
Ruvuma River, xi

Said bin Said, Seyyid, 106-7, 109-11
Salala, Emir of, 31
Salisbury, Lord, 41
Schaeffer, Colonel, 62
Schweinfurth, G., 46, 56
Scott, J., 33
Sebehr Rahama, 56-8
Sennar, 52, 55, 63
Seward, G. E., 23
Seychelles, 9, 86-7
Shilluk, 45, 74
Ships:

    Albacore, 70
    Ariel, 91